I could scarcely put this bo
and missteps of the early da, ... p........ ...., ...
the glories of wisdom, perseverance and hope that gradually
emerges. No matter what your pastoral setting, this book
will help you get – or stay – on the paths of righteousness.

Greg Scharf
Pastor for 25 years,
Professor of Pastoral Theology,
Trinity Evangelical Divinity School, Deerfield, Illinois

This heart-warming (and at times heart-wrenching) story
of the downs and ups of ministry and church life offers the
kind of practical and godly wisdom that will help pastors
(and those they shepherd) towards a realistic appreciation
of what really matters as we serve Christ and his people.

John Woodhouse
Principal of Moore College,
Sydney, Australia

I didn't think I would like this book, but as I read my way
into it, it seemed to resonate with reality. So much so that
I plan to commend this book to our students here at Beeson
Divinity School and to pastors everywhere who are called
to the burdensome joy of shepherding the flock of God.

Timothy George
General Editor of the *Reformation Commentary on Scripture*,
Founding Dean,
Beeson Divinity School, Samford University,
Birmingham, Alabama

This is a book that ought to be read not only by everyone in, or preparing for, pastoral ministry; but also by every church member who wants an insight into the ups and downs of their pastor's life. It highlights central principles of ministry, is full of good advice for a multiplicity of difficult pastoral situations, warns of temptations and snares as well as sharing with us the happier occasions of ministry, and all in the highly readable style of a series of email exchanges. Read it and discover why 'Everyone needs an Eldon.'

Hector Morrison
Principal of Highland Theological College,
Dingwall, Scotland

In this earthy and attractive page-turner of a book, we are exposed to the whole fascinating range of church life and Christian ministry, joys, scandals and all.

Richard Bewes
OBE, former Rector of All Souls Church,
Langham Place, London

Convicting, compelling and ultimately uplifting; this insightful probing of the realities of pastoral ministry will make you laugh, lead you to pray, and encourage you to persevere.

Colin S. Smith
Senior Pastor of The Orchard Evangelical Free Church,
Deerfield, Illinois
President of *Unlocking the Bible*

Pastoring
the
Pastor

Emails of a Journey Through Ministry

Tim Cooper and Kelvin Gardiner

CHRISTIAN
FOCUS

Tim Cooper lives with his wife Kate and their four sons in Dunedin, New Zealand. He is Senior Lecturer in the History of Christianity in the Department of Theology and Religion at the University of Otago. Before taking up this post he was the pastor of LifeSwitch, a church in the Hutt Valley on the outskirts of Wellington, New Zealand's capital city.

Kelvin Gardiner has pastored churches in New Zealand (Rutland St. Church in Christchurch), the Philippines (Capitol City Baptist Church West Avenue Quezon City) and the US (North Seattle Alliance Church). For ten years he led a ministry leadership organization overseeing one hundred US churches and providing pastoral support for overseas mission teams. He and his wife Jill currently offer pastoral care for mission agencies in Asia and Europe.

Copyright © Tim Cooper and Kelvin Gardiner 2012

ISBN 978-1-84550-784-8

Published
by
Christian Focus Publications
Geanies House, Fearn, Ross-shire,
IV20 1TW, Scotland

www.christianfocus.com

Cover design by Daniel van Straaten

Printed by
Bell and Bain, Glasgow

CONTENTS

To the community of believers at LifeSwitch
who taught me so much
and who held me with an open hand
(TIM COOPER)

To the pastors and people of Alaska and the US Pacific Northwest
who journeyed with me through joys and sorrows
learning so much more about ourselves and our faithful God
(KELVIN GARDINER)

Our thanks to Ken Edgecombe and Lynne Baab
who made this a better book.

Preface

I very nearly didn't survive at all. I had no idea that pastoral ministry was going to be this hard. I suppose I should have paid more attention. I certainly went in there with plenty of reading, thinking and training behind me. Perhaps I missed the part where they warned me just how difficult it would be. Perhaps I was too wrapped up in myself, in my hopes and ambitions; trusting to a self-confidence that seemed so robust at the beginning, but proved to be brittle, fragile, vulnerable – like the topping on a crème brulée, firm on the surface but all custard beneath. Or perhaps there really is no adequate preparation. The rhythms of ministry may be so foreign and strange that there is no way of truly understanding them except by living in them. They were nearly the end of me.

I know this seems bleak, even hopeless, and that's not what I want to convey. I simply want to start at the beginning. I want to be honest. It is true that my adjustment to full-time ministry in the local church has been the most traumatic experience of my life. Yet now, standing in this place, I wouldn't have missed it for anything. There have been wounds, for sure, but there have also been precious moments, deep life-giving instalments in something much bigger than we can ever see. I have never grown so much, never seen so much – in myself, or in God's great purposes in the world. I have gained, and now all the pain and bewilderment I went through seems a small price to pay. In the end, I survived.

I have my Uncle Eldon to thank for that. He was God's blessing and gift to me, just when I needed him. I truly believe that his wisdom made all the difference – seemingly unending layers of insight born of decades of experience of these disorienting rhythms. They grounded me. Sometimes his words were personal and painful (the wounds of a friend) but they gave me the understanding I so desperately needed. They gave me hope. They gave me life.

It didn't take long for me to work out that I couldn't keep his wisdom to myself, and that is why this little book now sits in your hands.

At first I thought I could summarize all that he had passed on to me in my own words. I spent months writing and deleting, wandering around in circles. Finally I realized that I was going about it the wrong way. His wisdom wasn't mine to give. It had to come in his own words, though by then it was too late for that. I was on the verge of giving up when my wife Hayley offered one of her marvellous, timely suggestions: I could recapture his words precisely, by reassembling the many emails he had sent me.

The project grew from there, and so did my excitement. First I rounded up all of his messages. Some had gone missing, but I found most of them sitting in my archive. Even by themselves they would have been brilliant. But I saw they needed context – I would have to include my own messages to him. I was reluctant at first, because if I'm honest I'm embarrassed by so many of my emails, especially the earlier ones. I didn't see then just how self-absorbed I was, how naïve, how puffed up with pride and arrogance. But as painful as they are for me to read now, I have chosen to include them as they were, without any editing or tampering. I hope I have learned by now that my reputation is of little consequence, but I also hope you will see how I changed and grew.

To my surprise, when others discovered what I was doing they asked to be involved. Martha Krinks was an ally of mine from the very start. She allowed me to look through her own archive to find emails that shed light on my experience. I have included some of those, thinking it will help if you gain a sense of how other people have registered my presence here in Broadfield. Harry Compton also offered me some of his messages. He was most definitely not an ally from the beginning, but I will let his emails tell you that story. I am grateful to everyone here at Broadfield Community Church, for their patience with me, and for their willingness to let this story be told. I am especially thankful to Sam Campbell. He has graciously and humbly allowed his emails to be included – his experience may serve as a form of salutary wisdom in its own way. The only names I have changed, to preserve anonymity, are those of the Murkowskis. When you read what they did, I think you will understand why. But apart from that I have left all these emails exactly as they were written.

So here they are. If you do not serve in pastoral ministry, my hope is that you will gain a glimpse of what life is like for those who do. As I said, you really have no idea how hard it is except by doing it, so perhaps you will be more generous and understanding as a result of seeing what it was like for me. The details may be different, but I'm sure the patterns are pretty much the same the world over. This work is not nearly as easy as it might look from the outside. And if you are in ministry, you know that already. I hope you will find here the wisdom you require to help you see more clearly, just as I did.

Everyone needs an Eldon; may you find yours. But if there is not one at hand, you can borrow mine. May you find in these pages what I found when I first opened up each new message. I still recall my delight and anticipation (and often relief) each time I saw my uncle's name in the inbox. And I still gain from the promise each one delivered. May you find that promise too: life, hope, encouragement, and the determination to carry on to the fullness of all that God has called us to be.

Daniel Donford
Broadfield

Beginnings

Daniel Donford

From: daniel@hubris.com
Sent: Tuesday 4 June, 11:23 a.m.
To: eldon@charis.net
Subject: Exciting News!

Dear Uncle Eldon,

Guess what! I am now a pastor. Like you all those years ago, I have said 'yes' to a church. My name will be on the weekly bulletin. I will stand in the pulpit each Sunday and preach. I will counsel and lead God's people. I will bless their babies, marry their children, and bury their loved ones. I will be the one they turn to for spiritual help. I am so excited. Could you have ever thought that of all the members of the extended family, I would be the one God would call to follow you into ministry? Me! The one my parents despaired of because I always had my nose in a book and never took to sports like the others, the one whose school reports nearly always mentioned something about being socially naïve or a dreamer! Now here I am. A leader. A pastor. My mother has always looked up to you – not just as her brother – and now I'm joining you in the same work. It feels good.

Thanks again for your support along the way. I can still remember you telling me to be patient while I waited to get into seminary, but that wasn't easy. You know me, once I get something in my mind I just have to do it. And then I interviewed you about your ministry over at Camden. Thirty-eight years in the same place! It was so inspiring to hear all that was going on there. I couldn't wait to be doing the same things myself. Well, now I can!

I think I told you about the options I had. I decided that Crater's Creek was just too remote. I don't think I'm cut out for rural living. I remember that summer on Uncle Bert's farm and I still feel tired when I think about it. I just couldn't cope with the early mornings. South Thornton didn't appeal much either. The church building was too small and my office was way round the back where it would never get any sun. That left Eversdale, but I didn't much care for the head of their search committee. If I don't warm to him, how will I warm to the whole church? So, as I think I was saying to you, I was feeling a bit stuck. All my other friends have found pastorates and it looked like I might miss out.

Then, just yesterday, I got a letter from Broadfield! I'd almost forgotten about them. It's a city of about eighty thousand or so. That's important to me – there has to be big potential for growth. Sydney Schneider's latest book is good on this – have you read it yet? He says a church in any town with less than fifty thousand people will struggle to get to the size it needs to be. So this one should fit just fine. Broadfield Community Church has only about a hundred members at the moment and there are only eighty-four other churches in the town, so that should leave more than enough room for expansion.

I'm very grateful for your offer to give advice now and then but I'm not sure I'll need to take you up on it. I've read every single one of Schneider's books and I think he's covered all the bases (not to mention all my seminary training). I should be well equipped by now, don't you think? I've practically memorized Schneider's *Church Growth In Four Easy Steps*. I was up till one o'clock this morning working with his templates. By my calculations I should be able to get Broadfield up to about two hundred members in my first year, though we'll need a bigger building to put them in. I'm praying for five-hundred in five years. As Schneider says, I should dream big dreams and see what God will do!

Everything is coming together nicely. Hayley is happy with the choice. It's further away from her mother but she's prepared to make the sacrifice. Emily will be starting school soon so the timing is right, and apparently Broadfield has some great schools. The church has an old parsonage right next door, which will be handy for Hayley. If David needs his day sleep on a Sunday she can bring him across early.

So I put my acceptance letter in the mail today. I'm very excited. I really sense God's leading. Working in a bookstore was okay but it wasn't very fulfilling in the end. I just can't wait to start working with Christians, to serve in a place that is characterized by love and unity and praise to God, a place where everyone treats you kindly. Last night I fell asleep dreaming of what it will be like to bring the saints together and lead them into a better future. Great things are ahead, I know it!

So, that's me. I thought you might like to know what I've decided. Feel free to come and visit any time, and I'll make sure Hayley adds your name to our newsletter list.

Please give my best wishes to Aunt Ethel.

Dan

Harry Compton

From: hjcompton@compton.com
Sent: Sunday 9 June, 1:34 p.m.
To: murkowskis@griblet.org
Subject: Fix it!

Tony

The chainsaw you sold me still isn't working properly.

I know you wanted to start a new life after all your disappointment. But I don't know why you bought into a chainsaw supply.

I'm sending it back again. Get it fixed this time.

Just got announced today. Another pastor. I met this one a couple of months ago. Wet as the new spring rains. I don't know what old Frank is thinking. I give this new guy three months, tops.

Harry

Martha Krinks

From: martha_krinks@endora.com
Sent: Tuesday 20 August, 10:36 a.m.
To: jdandemtrout@vmail.org
Subject: Life

My dear Janice,

Well now, I have just shuffled Stafford out the door to work, tidied the house some, then made myself a drink to have one of our nice little 'chats', though my coffee went cold while I tried to remember how I am supposed to work this computer. I have asked Stafford for help a few times but I am sure he thinks I am a hopeless case. I used to be so capable at this sort of thing in the days before I had children, you know, when I worked in George Maloney's legal firm. All I had was my typewriter. Now even my typing skills are rusty and I'm always making mistakes and having to go back and retype things. Oh well. Thanks for convincing me to sign up. My life is full enough even though the boys have all left home, but I like the new interest of using a computer. I can't believe I have my very own email address. It is so wonderful to come to my inbox every morning and see if there is mail. I sure get a thrill when I get a message from you. And it is so lovely to hear of your own dear family and that everything else up there in Fairview is going so smoothly.

Things are fine here in Broadfield as well, though to be honest I am just not too sure about our new pastor. His name is Daniel. Did I tell you about him? He arrived about a month ago I guess. He is kind of tall and pretty slim. I think his wife makes sure he dresses well. (Her name is Hayley and she is just the sweetest little thing you'll ever meet.) He has a full head of dark hair (almost black) and he wears glasses which make him look quite studious. He takes them off when he preaches. It is funny but those are the moments when he seems to shine. I sit there and just enjoy what he has to say. I try to smile whenever he looks at me, to give him some encouragement. The Lord knows he needs it. I have not talked about him too much with Stafford, but I think he wonders if they made the right choice. I suppose it is times like these when Stafford feels the weight of Eldership the most. He and Carlton do their best, don't they, but it is not easy. Not with Frank always around and not when their latest choice of pastor is off to such a shaky start. He is a dear when it comes to his preaching, but when it comes to other settings, I guess he seems arrogant to people and the way he tries to get us all excited about his new ideas just hasn't gone down well. He doesn't realize that he needs to give us time to know him and to understand him, he just rushes off ahead of us and doesn't stop to look behind much. But, as my mother used to say, 'Always look for the best in people', and when I do that, I think I can see that he's just eager and unsure and a little threatened and inexperienced. Actually he's really quite likeable. But he has got a lot ahead of him, that's all I can say. So I pray for him and bake him cakes and give him every little encouragement whenever I can.

Look at the time! I'm supposed to be out at a Bible study at eleven. I had better hurry on. But it is so lovely to talk to you. I will be sure to keep you posted on how things are going here.

Do give my love to Ed.

Martha

Daniel Donford

From:	daniel@hubris.com
Sent:	Monday 14 October, 6:14 a.m.
To:	eldon@charis.net
Subject:	Help!

Dear Uncle Eldon,

Church is miserable! I've been here three months now and things are not what I expected! Do you remember offering to send me advice whenever I needed it? Well, I need it now! Can you help????

Dan

Changes

Daniel Donford

From:	daniel@hubris.com
Sent:	Tuesday 15 October, 9:08 a.m.
To:	eldon@charis.net
Subject:	Help!!

Oh Uncle Eldon!

I'm in trouble. I'm in so much trouble! I can barely bring myself to describe it. You remember those heavy old blankets Aunt Ethel used to throw over our beds when we came to stay. It feels like twenty – no fifty! – of those have been piled up on my shoulders so that I can't even walk. I stumble along in the gloom, weighed down and anxious.

The fact is, I made a mistake. Well, someone did, either me or God. And since I still manage to believe that God doesn't make mistakes, I suppose it was me. I can't understand it. I was so sure of God's leading. I knew that he wanted me to be here. But I know it's not going to happen. I just know. I should have gone to South Thornton. Better a cold office than this nightmare.

I can't say how relieved I am that you're still willing to help me out. It's humiliating to admit that I've come unstuck so quickly, but I don't know what else to do.

Where do I begin? I don't know. I don't even want to think about it. But if I have to, let me introduce you to Frank Schumacher. I've made the unhappy discovery that everything around here (everything!) begins and ends with him. He must be consulted on all matters. I didn't meet him when we came for the interview. No doubt he lurked in the background, darkly plotting. But he runs the place, he really does, even though he retired from Eldership over five years ago. He looks about 140 years old, with eyes of forged steel. He stands as stiff as a board, and he's over six feet tall. Every time I preach he just stares at me, when he's not reading his Bible and working out all the scriptural reasons why I'm wrong. He quotes the Bible like he wrote it himself.

Anyway, our Elders. There are two of them. It turns out that Carlton Stockard is Frank's son-in-law. I almost feel sorry for him – when I'm not mad at him. Just when I think we've agreed on something, off he runs to Frank who shoots it down. He has no backbone. And his wife Annie doesn't want to stand up to her father either. What chance do I have?

The other Elder is Stafford Krinks. He's a nice enough guy and his wife is positively delightful (to be honest, she's the only one who's been even remotely friendly to me). I think he wishes things were different. But he hasn't got what it takes to stand up to Frank. No one has, that's the problem. Apparently, Frank's grandfather bought the land the church was built on and he provided the materials. No one says as much, but it's clear to me that this is Frank's church and everybody knows it. That probably explains why they've had eight pastors in the last twelve years – a fact that no one mentioned to me at the interview. How can I possibly succeed where so many others have so miserably failed?

It might be okay if Frank Schumacher was my only problem, but he's not. Just when you thought it wasn't possible for anyone to be older than Frank, there's Harold Carmichael. Ever since I got here he's been determined to come round and see me to 'talk things through'.

Uh uh! He reminds me too much of Frank, except he's a whole lot shorter and has a glass eye that stares off in another direction entirely. (He's been widowed for decades and lives at home alone with his dog. Apparently it's one of those tiny breeds that's basically a glorified rat and it has only one eye as well. Talk about dogs looking like their masters!) Mostly I try to avoid him. Last time I put him off by saying I had to take Emily to a ballet lesson. Emily doesn't even know what ballet is. Can you believe it? I actually lied!

And then there's Doris Blackmore. She also reminds me of Frank, though she's about a hundred years younger. In church she sits with her husband, Andrew, and they have these whispered arguments. But all through my sermons she fixes me with this angry gaze. What have I done to her! Why is everyone determined to send me away?

Well, if that's what they want, they can have it. I haven't mentioned everything, but you get the picture. I'm in the wrong place. Now what do I do?

Your loving, desperate nephew,

Dan

Harry Compton

From: hjcompton@compton.com
Sent: Tuesday 15 October, 5:37 p.m.
To: murkowskis@griblet.org
Subject: Progress

Tony

I'm pleased to hear you're still interested in pastoring this place. I know there's some bad history between you and Broadfield, or between you and Frank. It's time to put that aside. The new boy is out of his depth and floundering. I don't think he'll last much longer. Frank will push him out soon. Maybe this is your chance.

Harry

Uncle Eldon

From:	eldon@charis.net
Sent:	Tuesday 15 October, 8:13 p.m.
To:	daniel@hubris.com
Subject:	Re: Help!!

Dan:

Thanks so much for emailing me a few months ago and again today. As I said yesterday, I am here to help. In fact, I wanted to reply after your very first email but I'm glad I waited as your communication today gives me the opportunity to speak about several things.

So you've hit some major roadblocks in ministry and are wondering if you've made a mistake in moving to Broadfield. Welcome to the realities of ministry. You are now experiencing the pain of unfulfilled expectations. It certainly sounds as if this man Frank is the ultimate controller and the two Elders are unable or unwilling to stand against his tactics. I am sorry. If only they would change their behaviours, your joy would return and there would be some chance of you leading the church along the path you have planned. I have met their kind many times along the years of ministry and could give you what I think are good suggestions for bringing about change in their attitudes and behaviour.

But if you don't mind, I'll leave that for another day. Right now I would like to turn the spotlight off them and turn it towards you. I hate to say it but there are two sides to every issue and, as hard as it is, I have found that focusing honestly on my side first has always been a major factor in effective resolution of problems. I guess that's because all of us are able to make changes in our own lives, but we are unable to impose our will on others to change them.

First let's review what you have told me, from your earlier email. There are some words there that need to come under scrutiny. Dan, God has called you to use the incredible gifts He has given you for His glory. Your heart is towards Him, and I am thrilled to see the way you have obeyed His leading into vocational ministry. I am saddened that so soon into the journey you are writing words like 'I stumble along in the gloom, weighed down and anxious, I made a mistake, it's humiliating, if I go on much longer it will kill me'.

Well, the good news is it won't kill you. It may hurt for a while, but if your eyes are turned towards the Lord, you will grow through the pain. Might it be that the things that are 'killing' you are actually caused in good measure by your eyes not being focused fully on the Lord? In your excitement of describing how you have come to be in ministry in Broadfield, you have revealed your heart, and the words you are writing are saying, 'it's all about me'. Please don't delete me to the trash bin just yet. Look at what you wrote in that first email. There's little about waiting on the Lord and spending extended times of prayer, but a lot about your decisions and feelings. (Since when did God promise you an office that got the sun?) There's little about reading the Word and times of meditating that provided God with the opportunity to burn certain verses into your heart. It sounds as if you've taken your guidance from Schneider's books and while he is a man whom God has blessed incredibly in ministry, he is writing about methods that have worked for him, but they may have worked for him because he first did what

I'm suggesting you do now, and that is tuning your heart to the principles of ministry. And the first principle is that who you are is far more important than what you do. Your identity in Christ is the foundation of your ministry life. If you are not able to rest in the sufficiency of Christ for everything in your life, you will quickly resort to finding your identity in what you do for Him, and right now you have to admit that that is looking pretty horrible. Broadfield Community Church is not a problem for you to fix, it is a community of people for you to love in the name of Christ, and shepherd in the ways that He has for them. Rest in the Lord and be His man in ministry and I predict you will have a life of joy at the deepest level; try to manipulate the church to fit your dreams and your life of misery has only just begun.

Sorry to be so blunt, but I want you to finish well, and that requires starting well. I do like those verses in Job 23 where Job says that he is looking for God in the east, west, north, and south, and not seeing Him. And then these words: 'I cannot see Him but He knows the way I take. When He has tried me He will bring me forth as gold'. Don't blame God for the situation you have got yourself into, but know that He was not caught by surprise. You may not see Him in this, but He sees you and knows the path you are on. The testing He is allowing will produce qualities in you that are like gold in His hands. Stay the course. Keep your eyes on Jesus. Make your relationship with Him your first priority.

If you want, I can give you some thoughts on how to work with the people in the church that are causing you grief. Let me know.

Be assured of my prayers for you, my love for you, and my desire to see you grow more and more like Christ in the days ahead.

Eldon

Daniel Donford

From:	daniel@hubris.com
Sent:	Thursday 24 October, 2:43 p.m.
To:	eldon@charis.net
Subject:	Thanks, I Guess

Dear Uncle Eldon,

I know it's taken me some time to come back to you, but, I have to be honest, I thought you were pretty hard on me in your email. The thing is, you just don't know these people! If you were actually here you'd see what I mean. They're awful, really they are! No one is my own age. No one seems to like me all that much. What have I ever done to them except to turn up and try to help them get with it?

Perhaps a parable will help you to understand what I'm dealing with. Most mornings I hear a series of loud cracks on the roof of our conservatory. It's a crow cracking open the shell of a snail to eat its innards. The meaning? Frank and I are both in that parable and I'll give you a clue: I'm not the bird. I don't have the beady eyes for it. Or the beak. Every conversation with Frank fractures my shell just a little more. Soon he'll suck the life right out of me.

So perhaps you could give me the suggestions you mentioned about how to deal with these people. I really don't see why all your advice had to be just for me.

Oh, this will help too. Did I tell you about the church meeting we had? Did I? I don't think I did. This was one Sunday after church, a week or two after we arrived. I wanted to let them know what the Lord had laid on my heart, so I told them. I painted this amazing picture of how God could turn the place around, clear out the cobwebs and actually connect with the community – that sort of thing. Well, you'd think I insulted their mother. No one seemed comfortable. Some people even refused to look at me. When I finished, there was this ghastly silence. Then Frank Schumacher suggested that we move onto the next item of business. (I nearly said, 'You mean writing the obituary for this church', but I didn't.) No one backed me up. No one. They hurried through everything else and nobody has talked about it since. Now I reckon they look at me sideways, except for Doris Blackmore who is always ready to stare me in the eye. Have they rejected me before I've even begun?

What do I do? I'm all for reading my Bible and seeking the Lord – I've done that, even if I didn't mention it in my earlier message – but I don't see how that's going to help their stubbornness. Please, please give me the advice you promised.

Yours, in dire need,

Dan

Daniel Donford

From:	daniel@hubris.com
Sent:	Thursday 24 October, 8:46 p.m.
To:	eldon@charis.net
Subject:	You're Right

Dear Uncle Eldon,

I'm really sorry for my earlier email. I should never have sent it, I can see that now.

It's been some afternoon. Hayley was emailing a friend and she happened to read what I wrote to you. She stopped what she was doing and tracked me down. We haven't had a conversation like that one in a long time, but I guess it's what I needed to hear. I suppose you can imagine it. She said she thought you were right on the money and that I should listen to you. She's been worried for a while that I'm more interested in Schneider's books than reading the Bible (but then, she's never much cared for him). She wonders if I've gotten distracted from what's really important and, well, to use her words, a bit puffed up. (Ouch!)

That was tough to take so, to recover, I went for a long walk. I didn't get far. There are some woods near our home with a small lake that is so peaceful. It has a promontory with a large boulder at the end that has been worn down in layers to provide several comfortable places to sit. Sometimes I choose that spot, or there's a tree just along the shore. Rather than having one trunk it has about ten that have coiled outwards over the years. When the leaves are full I can sit up there and not be seen, unless someone is standing right under me. Today I chose the tree, trying to hide. I sat there with my legs dangling over the water, praying and reflecting. That was pretty tough, too. The more I thought about it the more I saw that you're right. It's been all about me, and not much about God or even the people in the church. I must admit, I felt like quite a failure.

But when I got home, there was the box of books you sent, waiting for me on the doorstep! I nearly cried when I saw who they were from. You are so generous. The titles sound like just what I need. They will be good for my heart. I'd start reading them right now, but I feel wrung out. I'll start tomorrow.

So I need to get some sleep. It's been a tough day, and right now I feel tired and dispirited. But I didn't want to end the day without writing to you first. If I could call back my earlier message I would. Can you delete it? I know I have to look to the problems in me first, but if you have some suggestions for how to handle this situation, I'd love to hear them.

Yours, with gratitude,

Dan

Uncle Eldon

From: eldon@charis.net
Sent: Friday 25 October, 2:34 p.m.
To: daniel@hubris.com
Subject: Re: You're Right

Dan:

So you thought I was a little tough on you in my last email? And then you apologized for saying so. I appreciate your honesty and I want you to know that I will try to never say anything with the intention of hurting you. Everything should be directed at some issue of ministry. Some words may hurt, not because they attack you personally but because they address something in your approach to ministry that might need to change. It's a principle you might want to adopt in your own ministry. Of course if I see serious character flaws emerging, I won't keep silent.

Having said that, I do want to encourage you to keep sharing your feelings. Holding back frustration or anger doesn't facilitate growth in the Christian life.

Actually, when I read your account of the church meeting my mind went to Psalm 42 where the writer is in exile. He apparently was the worship leader back in the good times but now he has no building, no people to lead, and no song to sing. Where is God when it hurts? But midway through the Psalm he changes significantly and describes the waves and billows crashing over him as 'yours' (that is, God's). God is allowing this trouble to come on him and that in turn makes him understand that God's presence is more important than the circumstance. So he can end the Psalm with the assurance that he will again praise God for the help of His presence. Outwardly the circumstances were the same – still no building, no people, no song – but inwardly everything had changed. I have gone back to that Psalm many times during my ministry days.

Now here's the specific advice you were asking for, but note that it is coming more slowly than you want. I won't be hurried on this because I have learned the hard way that there is no formula for a quick fix of trouble in a church. It's a journey. And the journey is primarily about your personal walk with the Lord.

I would suggest starting with the two other Elders as they will be your greatest allies once they know you and trust you. Build relationships with them by spending time together, in your home and theirs, learning all about their lives with its joys and heartaches. Every time you are with them, no matter how informal or casual the setting, take time to pray together. Anchor your relationship in the desire you share with them to honour God in every aspect of your lives.

Next I would spend significant time getting to know the congregation. Go to them as individuals and families and listen to their stories. Find out where they have come from. What are their current dreams and hopes? How did they come into the family of God? What would they like to see the church become in five years? Tell them that we don't live in isolation and we need each other. Ask them what their expectations are for you. It's going to take some time and you will see how different people are. You will also see how diverse are the ways that our God works in people's lives, and how we need to be careful not to box the people we serve into our own narrow containers.

Which leaves me with one more thought for today. At the church meeting you describe 'painting this amazing picture of how God could turn the place around, clear out the cobwebs and actually connect with the community.' Well, the good news is that apparently God laid it on your heart. The bad news is they didn't see the picture you painted, or the cobwebs that need to be cleared out. So in effect you did, in your own words, 'insult their mother'. They like the church the way it is and are offended by your criticism. It won't have a long-term negative effect if you are willing to admit you spoke in haste and without regard for their feelings. Saying sorry is a good thing if you mean it, and if they can see that you like them the way they are before you try to change them towards a future they don't yet see.

I haven't talked about Frank the controller, but I will when I sense the time is right. I suggest you might do the same, and concentrate on those who are more important right now, Elders and the families of the church.

Keep me informed, I am cheering you on.

Eldon

PS, Enjoy the books I sent but don't see them as a source of solutions. They will fit best in your ministry tool kit when you are trusting the Lord for the help you need. And listen to Hayley. Your wife can read you 'like a book'.

Daniel Donford

From:	daniel@hubris.com
Sent:	Thursday 31 October, 12:26 p.m.
To:	eldon@charis.net
Subject:	Thanks!

Dear Uncle Eldon,

You are so gracious! Thanks for putting up with me. There's not too much of that around here, so I'm grateful to find it in you. It's a relief to have someone to talk to. Between you and Hayley I have some good company on this journey. You say listen to her, and she says listen to you, so I guess I'm stuck between the two of you. Which means I'm not quite as alone as I thought.

I'm following your advice, by the way, though I did wonder at your approach. If Frank Schumacher is the big problem around here, why not start with him? What was the point of cultivating my relationship with Carlton and Stafford if it's all going to bounce back off Frank? Then again, I'm going to need their support when it comes to the inevitable confrontation, which will make it worth the effort. So do give me your thoughts on him when you sense the time is right, which I hope is in your next email. The man really is intolerable, you know. Everyone else refers to me as 'our pastor', but Frank speaks my name as if he's talking through a bar of soap. He's so patronizing, but when I talk to him my confidence vanishes, words forsake me and he defeats me every time. It wakes me up at nights. My stomach begins to churn and I start to rehearse conversations with him. I go over them and over them. Some aren't pretty. Have you noticed how everything seems so much worse in the middle of the night? So the coward in me is quite happy to delay the day when I confront Frank over his issues. In the meantime I'm practicing for it in my head.

But I've been trying to do what you said. I think you'll be pleased with me. It all stemmed from Sunday morning, which was my lowest point so far. I was walking into the service late (I'd left some notes in my office) when I saw this guy hanging around outside, looking at our noticeboard. I asked him if he was interested in coming in. He said that he'd been wondering about this 'God thing' and whether he should check out a church. I almost sent him to the one around the corner (that's where I'd go if I wasn't working here) but decided against it. So I brought him in for what was by no means our worst service ever, but it was bad enough. I didn't realize that I'd parked him behind Andrew and Doris Blackmore, who bickered with each other through the whole service, apart from those intervals when Black-looks Blackmore stared at me in stony silence while I preached. All through the sharing time I was so conscious of how this guy would see it, which was very painful. Everyone used words that would mean nothing to him. We sang these songs that were so way out – I swear they were all at least a thousand years old. I realize how it all would have shut him out, distanced him. I'm sure it was entirely irrelevant to the world as he knew it.

He hurried out at the end, but I managed to catch him in the foyer. He explained that he liked my sermon and everything, but if he had to be like 'these people' to follow God he wasn't interested. Before I could agree with him, Harold Carmichael burst in on us. He stood in my face and asked when he could come round to 'talk about things'. I came very close to throttling him, but that would have been a pretty bad witness. Then he noticed this guy and said, 'Well, young man, where do you fellowship?' I could hardly breathe, let alone speak. The guy just gave me this bemused look and walked out the door. I doubt he'll ever go back to any church now, let alone ours.

I'm sure you can appreciate how discouraged I was. I was still in the dumps yesterday afternoon when Stafford came round to drop off some papers for tonight's Elders' meeting. He was just about to leave when I recalled your advice, so I invited him to go for a walk with me. We went around to that lake I told you about and sat on the boulder. I shared with him my sadness about Sunday. He had sensed something was going on, and he wasn't surprised. Actually, I was impressed by his insight and understanding. We talked for a good hour or two. It didn't solve anything, but it brought us closer together and I was strangely encouraged by the end of it.

Hayley's calling me for lunch now. Since you've told me I have to listen to her, I'd better go…

Dan

Daniel Donford

From:	daniel@hubris.com
Sent:	Monday 18 November, 4:42 p.m.
To:	eldon@charis.net
Subject:	Meetings

Dear Uncle Eldon,

I've been holding off writing to you, but Hayley says that I have to. She never lets me do what I feel like doing these days. Like running off to the Bahamas or somewhere, and never coming back. She says I'll just be taking my problems with me, which seems crazy. If the problems are people then how can a desert island possibly throw them in my face all over again? I don't remember feeling like this before and it's a little scary. But now that I'm starting to tell you about it, I'm beginning to feel better. I guess it helps. (Hayley said that as well – when is she not right?)

Anyway, I have been reluctant to write to you because I don't want to face up to the fact that I'm hopeless at this pastoring business. Why is it that when I read what you say I get all inspired, and when I try to do it I fall flat on my face? Why do I feel positive about things one week, and so very bleak the next? You're not interested in a new position are you? I'm sure you'd do a much better job around here than I'm doing.

I've been feeling like this since our last church meeting. I thought several months was time enough for everyone to cool off and see things more clearly before I raised the subject of change again. The deacons had suggested replacing the drain that goes out to the road.

I took that as my chance to talk about other changes we could make to the place. I was careful not to be too scathing of the building (even if it does look like the architect had a drinking problem when he designed it). I simply suggested that if we knocked out one wall and extended the auditorium into the parking lot we could seat another 73 people. They looked at me with utter incomprehension. Do they have any vision at all? Do they want to grow?

Apparently not. No one backed me up. Harry and Jane Compton (some old hands) were practically shaking their heads, but they're hardly change agents. Harry's still wearing the same jacket he wore to church in 1978. And I'm not sure that he likes me very much. Doris Blackmore looked positively derisive. I sat there hoping that Carlton or Stafford would speak up, but before they got the chance Frank assumed command. The words he used are a blur now – I remember it all through a daze. I felt like the victim of an assault.

Anyway, the meeting was rapidly getting out of control. People looked ready to run and I would have joined them. Instead, I followed the first idea that popped into my head: I began quite a lengthy ramble on the glories of Christ. I could see that people were bewildered, but in an odd way it worked. Things calmed down and the discussion never got back to the subject of the building, which I think was a relief to us all. I didn't stop to talk to anyone on the way out. I hurried home, almost in tears, hoping they thought I was spiritually minded rather than desperately stupid.

And then! Oh, Uncle Eldon. The next day I went along to meet with the youth group. All six of them. They were having a study on dating, but one girl asked if I'd talk about the glories of Christ. She said it with such a serious expression I still don't know if she was mocking me. Worse still, at some point I must have streaked red whiteboard marker all down one side of my face. I never noticed, and they weren't going to tell me. I did wonder why they kept asking me what I thought about wearing makeup. It took Hayley to point it out to me when I got home. I nearly cried all over again. What a washout.

Perhaps that explains why I hesitated to report back to you. I'm a failure.

Dan

Harry Compton

From:	hjcompton@compton.com
Sent:	Monday 18 November, 11:57 p.m.
To:	murkowskis@griblet.org
Subject:	What's Going On?

Tony

I haven't heard from you. I hope you're not weaseling out of this. Soon he'll be gone and Frank will have someone else lined up. How will you get the job if you're not here to take it! Get a move on.

Harry

Uncle Eldon

From: eldon@charis.net
Sent: Tuesday 19 November, 8:44 a.m.
To: daniel@hubris.com
Subject: Re: Meetings

Dan:

I am sorry things appear to be going so badly for you in the church. It really must be hard going and I am praying that you will soon get beyond feeling hopeless as a leader, and that your ministry is a failure. Remember that God delights to use the weak and foolish to confound the strong and wise.

Perhaps it is time I said something about Frank. Nearly every church I know has at least one person with the need to control every decision and activity, particularly as they relate to change. You are obviously afraid of him as you describe him as 'intolerable, patronizing' and one who defeats you every time. Yet the day will come when I am confident you will write to tell me he is actually insecure, frightened about the future, and probably very lonely.

Some of the best advice I ever received was from a military man, highly decorated because of his bravery in leadership, and an Elder in his church. I still call him regularly as I encounter situations that I have never faced before, as his godly, sound advice has helped calm many a storm. He always has time for me, and even though he is younger than me, his life journey has taught him many things I have still to learn. If I told him about Frank, he would reply with one word: de-escalate. It's a word that is burned into my brain.

The Franks of this world claim their authority by loudly stating a position on an issue and daring those who think otherwise to enter dialogue. They believe that by speaking loudly and confidently, by invoking the fact that it has worked in the past, and by recruiting a few people of similar mind who can also speak loudly, they will win any debate. In a word, they know that the more they can escalate their issue and keep it on the table and in conversation, the more likely those who oppose it will lose heart and go home. They love it when people like you engage them over the issue. They have probably never considered the word or understood it but if they had, it would make them tremble. The word is de-escalate.

To de-escalate is to ignore their loud chatter and threats, it is to not reply to their written challenges, it is to change the subject when meeting face to face to talk about the attributes of God's grace or any of the 'whatsoever' things that are true and noble and of good report (Phil. 4). In a way, that's what you did in the meeting though I can see how people might have been mystified by your change of direction. Of course there will be a time when the subject has to be dealt with and then my advice is to restrict your speech to asking questions. Have Frank explain, clarify, and unwrap his point of view. Ask and ask again and see how his position falls apart as you refuse to push back with anything of your own point of view, but persistently and graciously ask for greater explanation of his. Don't let him get away with generalizations but insist on substance that will support his argument. Learning to ask good questions is the mark of a growing leader, and you will make greater progress in leadership by asking ahead of telling.

As you do this, find time to meet with him personally and listen to his life journey. As you ask questions in this area you will find his heart revealed to you, and discover the hurts and insecurities that lead to the behaviour you are seeing in him now. I can name a few Franks in my experience that became my greatest allies and closest friends as I learned to de-escalate their issues and love them as brothers in Christ. Sadly I can also name a few that I did not treat with grace, and the outcome was less desirable.

Be encouraged. God is for you, so is Hayley, and for what it's worth, so am I. That's three allies, and when one of them is God, I would say you are on to a good thing. Remember Him as 'your glory and the lifter of your head'.

Look Up!

Eldon

Daniel Donford

From:	daniel@hubris.com
Sent:	Sunday 30 November, 1:47 p.m.
To:	eldon@charis.net
Subject:	Preaching

Dear Uncle Eldon,

Thanks for your encouragement. I think I need a whole lot more of that right now. It's so deflating how I look forward to something, imagining how it's going to play out, and then when I get there it's entirely different. And when I get this sense that things aren't going how I expected, they steadily become less and less how I wanted and hoped.

Take this morning, for instance. Another Sunday at Broadfield under my illustrious leadership. I admit that usually I find preaching the most satisfying part of what I'm doing, but not this morning. The atmosphere among the congregation was noticeably stale, as if they were bored or distracted, though I couldn't tell you why. I thought I'd been doing okay and the service up to that point was interesting enough, to me at least. But ten minutes into my sermon I made a mistake – though it took me two minutes to realize.

We're in the middle of a short series on the fruit of the Spirit. I was making the point that the fruit is best seen in the community, not in the individual, since it requires the presence of others around us for our patience and love and faithfulness to be tested and demonstrated. I thought it was an excellent sequence of thoughts. Then I turned the page in my notes.

I don't know how this happened but that page was straight out of last week's sermon, not this week's. I did get an uneasy sense that something wasn't quite right as I couldn't recall that section when I had been going through my preparation earlier in the morning. Finally, I realized what had happened. I don't know what was more depressing – that I didn't notice I was re-preaching my own sermon or that no one else noticed that I had said all this just one week earlier. Not a single person looked quizzical or concerned. Only Martha Krinks gave me one of her smiles, but then she usually does whenever I look her way for more than a second or two. They all seemed to slumber on.

Well, I had little choice but to carry on myself, so I wove what I had said back into this week's sermon as best I could and we all went on our way. But as I was preaching I was also thinking: what good does preaching do? What difference does it actually make? When I look at the church from Sunday to Sunday I see precious little change to make me think it is worth all the agony and effort.

You have been doing this week in, week out for decades – you must have some idea. What keeps you preaching when as far as you can tell no one seems to be listening, really listening?

Dan

Uncle Eldon

From:	eldon@charis.net
Sent:	Sunday 30 November, 4:57 p.m.
To:	daniel@hubris.com
Subject:	Re: Preaching

Dan:

I see your email came just three hours ago which means you wrote it almost immediately after preaching to a 'slumbering' congregation as you call them. Bad timing. Probably better to have eaten a good lunch, watched some football on TV, taken the kids to the park, relaxed with Hayley and a good movie, then had a good night's sleep.

The mood on Monday is often better than Sunday.

But you asked, so I will answer. You had three questions about preaching:

1. What good does it do?
2. Does it make a difference?
3. Why is there no significant change in the congregation?

As an answer to Questions 1 and 2, I remind you that the Word of God is alive and powerful and able to penetrate to the core of our being. Not too many things in life have that sort of credential. The Word of God we read is like a hammer that breaks rock-like things in pieces, and it is like a sword that divides truth from error. And the preaching of the Word of God, when empowered by the Spirit of God, will achieve the purposes of God in individual lives.

The bottom line is that the good it does and the difference it makes are in the hands of God, and He promises if you preach, He will bless the lives of those who hear. That makes your third question almost irrelevant because while you may not see significant change in your people, God does, because He sees the heart, and heart change occurs before outward change becomes evident. The changes will eventually be seen, you need to be patient.

And you need to be ready to accept how those changes are reported. More often than not, affirmation of my preaching was directed to words I don't remember saying and points I am sure I never made. What I thought was the main point was clearly not God's main point, and He used His Word ahead of my words to effect the change He wanted in others.

It's interesting that this issue came up for you this week. Just days ago I received a note from someone who attended a conference I spoke at ten years ago. I remember the event but not what I said, but she does, including a detail which the Lord used to change her life. A decade later, she sent a kind letter. It is humbling that God used me that way and humbling that I can't claim any of the glory for something I don't remember. That's God's way.

Maybe preaching is as much (or more) about the preacher as it is about the congregation, so let me ask you about your preaching:

1. Is it doing you good?
2. Is it making a difference in your life?
3. Do your people see significant change in you?

Long ago, E.M. Bounds wrote, 'preaching is not perform-ance for an hour, it is the outflow of a life', and Jonathan Edwards the puritan preacher wrote, 'the Spirit first fills the life and that then fills the mouth'.

And if you will forgive me for returning to my constant theme that God is more interested in who you are than what you do, I think it also true that <u>He is more interested in developing messengers than messages</u>. I encourage you to refresh your soul when it comes to speaking the Word of God to the people. Let the Word speak to you, to hum-ble, refine, and deepen you, and then out of that experi-ence with Him, craft a message that speaks much of Him and little of you, so that the Holy Spirit can empower and bring fruit to the glory of God.

You are not charged with changing the disinterested listener, you are charged with proclaiming the Word of God in the power of the Spirit. We cannot save anyone, but He can. Give Him the opportunity to change the heart of stone to a heart of flesh, to divide truth from error, and to penetrate to the core of the most resistant heart. He can use you to do this, and when He does, you will give Him all the glory.

Tell me where to go to download your sermons and I will listen with an expectant heart.

Eldon

Martha Krinks

From: martha_krinks@endora.com
Sent: Sunday 1 December, 5:44 p.m.
To: jdandemtrout@vmail.org
Subject: Barn Dance

Dearest Janice,

Last night we had the most wonderful time out at Ted Saunders' farm on the edge of town. You remember the place – acres and acres of fields with his house and a lovely old big red barn plonked right there in the middle of it all. You really could not hope for a better setting, with hay bales all around the walls and straw on the floors. It wasn't the best weather for a barn dance but the place really warmed up and after a while it was possible to believe we might have been dancing on the hottest day of summer. It is such a joy to have a foretaste like that – I always think that is like a little glimpse of heaven ahead of time, just enough to give us the smallest sense of what it will be like. And to see so many people having so much fun. And you know how Stafford does like a barn dance. It takes away all his usual reticence. Sometimes I wonder who I am married to!

Though I have to share with you that I felt a tiny bit sad as well. When I looked all around those happy people I could see that nearly everyone from church was there, but dear Daniel and his lovely wife Hayley were not. I asked around to see if anyone had thought to invite them but it seems that no one had. I don't think it was deliberate. I do not think so many people would go out of their way not to include the pastor. Then again, the church does feel unsure about him and perhaps they are still reluctant to truly take him to heart.

I do feel for him because really he is doing his very very best. This morning he did something that I thought was so fresh and creative. I have never ever heard a preacher do anything like it before, and afterwards I wondered 'why not?', because I think it worked extremely well. Daniel was preaching away (on the fruit of the Spirit – an excellent series) when he began to repeat part of his message from last week. I didn't want to risk looking around to see if anyone else noticed and I am not sure they did – maybe the late night was too much for them. Anyway, there it was – exactly the same point that Daniel had made last Sunday. And I really did feel a stab in the heart because I thought that I should have listened to that last week and it was so effective for dear Daniel to speak it again because he must have known that we all needed it. I was going to thank him for it after the service but he slipped away quickly (as he sometimes does) and I didn't get the chance. But really I am so very encouraged. I do enjoy Daniel's preaching and it gives me hope that he might survive whatever trial he is going through at the moment. I only hope that others were paying attention as well.

Anyway I have a roast in the oven that I really must see to. Old Ted gave us a leg of lamb as we left, so I told him I would cook it up straight away and let him know how it tasted.

Give my love to Ed.

Martha

Daniel Donford

From:	daniel@hubris.com
Sent:	Friday 13 December, 3:16 p.m.
To:	eldon@charis.net
Subject:	Cats and Catastrophe

Dear Uncle Eldon,

I'm seriously beginning to worry that I'm not cut out for this pastoring business. I can't even get the pastoral visitation right.

On Sunday one of the people at Broadfield asked me to visit his aunt. I'd been thinking for a while that I should begin to visit people in their homes so I took that as a sign to start my glorious career in this great art. What a flop!

When the aunt in question – Meredith Bellweather – opened the door, she seemed the very definition of a sweet old lady. She was about five-foot-four, wearing denim jeans and a checked flannel shirt, which I suppose was normal enough. But there was a worrying smell of cats. Indeed, eighteen of them. She made a point of introducing me to each one individually. 'Here is Mildred', she said, and then she turned to me with an expectant look. There was an awkward few seconds while I waited for her to say something else, then she gave me an encouraging nod. Mildred looked up at me with baleful eyes. Meredith nodded again. Finally I realized that she wanted me to say hello to Mildred. So I did. Very uncomfortably. Fortunately there were only about a dozen of her cats around at the time and I think I was fairly used to it by the end. I gave the last one a little bow. Meredith chuckled. So far, so good.

Then she offered me a cup of tea. I don't like tea but I said yes anyway and she brought it out. I was just about to begin (not that I knew what to say) when she blurted out in a surprisingly loud voice, 'Spoons!' I began to say that I don't take sugar but she had disappeared into the kitchen. She came back with two large spoons, which she then proceeded to clink together on her knee with disconcerting exuberance. This went on for nearly a minute before she burst out with a very loud rendition of 'Onward Christian Soldiers'. Bemused, I looked away to see Mildred lapping at my tea. Then Meredith asked me to join her for the second verse. Did you know that hymn has five verses? It took me half an hour to get out of there.

It was Harry Compton who asked me to visit her. He seemed so sincere at the time, but now I'm not so sure.

Well, I didn't want to give up too early so I went on to my next appointment. A woman in the church had asked me to visit her brother. He has just lost his job at a local factory. I sat in his kitchen with him, utterly stuck for words. I didn't understand his world; he didn't understand mine. I had no idea how to encourage him. I left there as quickly as I could, without seeming rude. But it still felt awkward.

I had a third name on my list: Harold Carmichael. I had decided that I really did need to pay him the visit he had been nagging me about. But when I sat outside his house in my car, watching his little one-eyed dog scampering around the yard yapping at anyone passing by, all my resolve evaporated. I just couldn't face it. I felt like an actor who has forgotten his lines. Surely I had been taught something about this by someone, or read something. But right then I couldn't recall a thing.

Defeated, I went home early and told my woes to Hayley. She was sympathetic, but she laughed about the cats. Now when I'm sitting in my office she'll call out, 'Honey, come and say hello to Mildred!' It's taken me three days to find that even remotely funny.

If people are watching how I'm going, testing my capacities, I'm clearly not winning. Surely you have some advice?

Dan

Uncle Eldon

From:	eldon@charis.net
Sent:	Monday 16 December, 10:12 a.m.
To:	daniel@hubris.com
Subject:	Re: Cats and Catastrophe

Dan:

I agree with you when you say that visiting people can be one of the harder assignments as a new Pastor, but please don't use your experience with this group of three as your assessment for all pastoral visits. The 'cat' lady, a man who has no connection with (nor interest in) your church, and a church member who seems to have an agenda are not likely to be fertile fields for pastoral growth. You need to be proactive and choose some 'safe' people to visit first, those who will be happy for you to 'practice' what eventually will become one of the most satisfying aspects of ministry.

I suggest you make a list of the people in the church whom you would feel comfortable visiting and then prioritize them, starting maybe with the lonely, the elderly and those you know who are not expecting you to visit but who would be pleased to see you. Make sure the elderly folk are covered in a block, as I used to find there is competitiveness among them and a visit from the Pastor is something to be talked about. If you visited Mabel, you can be sure that Dorothy is hoping you won't be far away.

In my experience, your visit will be anticipated in at least four ways, and if you are aware of the possibilities, you can be better prepared.

Some people will have a sense of excitement that you are coming and so they will have plenty to say and more food ready than you need. They will want you to stay all day. Listen to them, you can tell them *your* story at a later time.

Others will be nervous of your coming, because they wonder what you might be asking or suggesting. A Pastor in the house is not the norm for them. You might have to take the lead in the conversation at first, by telling them something of your journey, showing them how ordinary you are, and steering them to talk about things comfortable to them. Go slow on religion and stay away from politics.

The hardest people for me to visit have been those who are shy and withdrawn. They are often known as godly, faithful, prayerful, gentle, but they sure aren't talkative. So it is very hard to gauge if you are being appropriate in what you are sharing with them. In the end, I developed a sort of routine that consisted of thanking them, affirming them, pointing them to Scripture that had recently been helpful to me, and then asking them to pray for me about some specific need. I said they were the hardest group at first, but looking back now I see they became the easiest over time because of their quiet and gentle spirit and their regular encouragement.

The last group I mention, and you can probably wait until you are more confident about this visiting business, are those I will call the critics or the cynics. They will tell you their history in the church, what is wrong with it, and how it could be fixed. Be gracious. Be careful. One of the techniques I employed was to ask them to write out their views and opinions, not with the prospect of adoption but for my greater understanding. Call for them to give biblical support, and hold them to being able to show that the current way is a violation of a biblical principle. Methods won't count for much in their calling for change, because effective church leaders will regularly be leading change in methods of the church. Principles on the other hand must not be changed or compromised.

End every visit by asking permission to pray for them. However you have been received, they know that a Pastor is a person who prays.

So start with safe people, then step out of your comfort zone and knock on some doors. You'll be glad you did.

Kind regards,

Eldon

Daniel Donford

From: daniel@hubris.com
Sent: Monday 6 January, 7:31 a.m.
To: eldon@charis.net
Subject: A Limerick

Exodus 2:15 –

There is a young pastor called Dan,
Who is doing the best that he can.
But it isn't enough,
And the going is tough:
To flee seems to be the best plan.

Uncle Eldon

From: eldon@charis.net
Sent: Tuesday 7 January, 6:47 a.m.
To: daniel@hubris.com
Subject: Re: A Limerick

Ephesians 6:13 –

There is a young pastor called Dan,
Who I'm sure is exactly the man
God has called to that place,
And he will by His grace
Endure, mature, and stand.

Martha Krinks

From: martha_krinks@endora.com
Sent: Thursday 16 January, 5:54 p.m.
To: jdandemtrout@vmail.org
Subject: Storm

Dearest Janice,

I have just heard on the radio that a winter storm is heading your way. I hope you are all prepared for it though I am sure you will be. You will have the cupboards stocked and a fire glowing and a brew of your pumpkin soup simmering away. I wish I could join you. The weather is not so bad here. They keep promising us some snow but it hasn't come yet. The nights are long and cold but we are keeping warm inside. Kevin and Sue have been gone a week now and the place seems so quiet without them and little Johnny. It was lovely having them here all through Christmas and the New Year celebrations. Grandchildren are such a delight, aren't they? I miss them so much but I know I can't hold onto them. I'll have to find someone else to mother I guess.

I suppose that's what I have been doing with our new pastor. He is not so new now but he still looks all lost at times. I just want to wrap him in my arms and give him a great big hug but I guess he wouldn't appreciate that very much now, would he? He and dear sweet Hayley came over for dinner the other night. After little Johnny had left I wanted to have some more children around to brighten up the house and Daniel and Hayley have two gorgeous little ones. They are just so cute. And it was good to welcome Daniel and try to give him something positive to think about for a change. I wonder if he doesn't like the winter months very much. You know how your cousin Sylvia used to get so down about things until they moved to Florida. Well I would not want Daniel to do that but he does seem so low sometimes. During the dinner it was as much as I could do to get two words out of him about the church. Stafford wanted to take the chance to talk through some of the things that are going on but Daniel just did not seem to respond. Hayley and I ended up discussing the children and little Emily's school and after a while Daniel began to ease up as well and we talked about football and the new town museum. He was almost laughing by the end which was just so wonderful to see.

I really do not know how he is going to get on. Between you and me, we are all bracing ourselves for losing another pastor and having to find a new one. I think we would all be very disappointed to have to do that because, you know, I really think Daniel might have it in him to do some good things. But he will need a lot of care and understanding and he is not really getting much of that. People wonder what is so hard about the job of pastor that he has to make it out to be so difficult. They just do not see things from his perspective I suppose and I don't think that he really understands theirs. I am quietly praying that God will give him all the strength and wisdom that he needs to get through. I know I am encouraging him on as best I can and I really think that others are too.

Well, I have a casserole that needs to come out of the oven. I hope the storm passes by without too much damage. I know you will cope well.

Give my love to Ed.

Martha

Daniel Donford

From:	daniel@hubris.com
Sent:	Friday 17 January, 10:16 a.m.
To:	eldon@charis.net
Subject:	Oppression

Dear Uncle Eldon,

I woke up this morning and realized that I'd lost something: my life. So much has changed. The whole pattern of my existence is different in ways I never expected. It used to be possible for me to allocate portions of my life to different categories: there was work, there was church, and outside of those two boxes there was life. But not anymore. Somehow the boundaries got washed away; separate streams converged into one. Now it's all over the place.

I don't have a church anymore – it's work. It's not the refuge that it once was. I'm too keyed up, too alert to what happens next, what people are thinking. It's impossible to relax in God's presence like I used to.

I don't have work either – it's church. I used to leave work behind at the office. Now I take it with me everywhere I go. Meetings happen at any time on any day. I miss the rhythm of the weekend – there is no weekend. I am on-call all the time, never entirely out of reach. It's relentless. The church always lingers in my shadow. There's no detaching it no matter how hard I try.

And there's no life – it's all work and church. When I go round to people's homes I can never rest easy. At some point – always, inevitably – people want to talk about the church. I know it's a passion for them, something they can bring out of its box and then put away again. But I can't. Even with Hayley, it's so hard to stop our conversations from drifting back around to the subject. It intrudes everywhere. I feel like I live my life handcuffed to an elephant. Everywhere I go, people ask me how my elephant is. Truth to tell, I'm sick of the elephant. I wish there was something else to talk about. But I can't get rid of it. It lurks in the background of all my relationships, all my conversations – everywhere. It's impossible to escape.

The other day I was standing in the pet food aisle at the supermarket. I was trying to explain to Emily why we couldn't possibly afford a cat. She wasn't paying much attention but I thought I was very convincing. The next thing I hear is, 'Don! Yoo hoo! Don!', and I turn around to find Meredith Bellweather peering over her trolley (she keeps calling me Don no matter how many times I tell her). Immediately I felt irritated though I tried not to show it, because it's really Harry Compton who is the problem. I've been told that he sends every new pastor around to visit his aunt as some sort of practical joke. So I talked to Meredith and tried to be pleasant, but all the time I was thinking: 'Is there no escape? Can I never get away?'

It's snowing heavily outside. The textured lawn, the crisp edgings and the banks of garden are beginning to disappear under a weight of snow that smothers all. I can't help feeling it's a picture of what's happening to my life. I'm being slowly buried. The oppression hangs over me like a black cloud. I have the sense of impending disaster all the time, like I'm hiking a mountain trail and a huge boulder is going to land on me just around the next corner. I can't quite see where the track is leading. And I've got all these people behind me, jostling and complaining. Last week I took Emily and David to play at the park at the north end of town. I mused while they played, thinking inevitably about church. I watched the trucks rumble past, envious of their drivers. There must be such freedom on the open road, just you sitting in the cab. No one to take along with you. Just uncomplaining freight silently going along for the ride. How different it is for me. If I'm going to get anywhere, I have to carry people with me. And that's harder than it looks. No one warned me it was going to be like this.

It might not be so bleak if I felt the least bit welcome here, but I don't. Things have gone so badly. I don't know what people think of me. It's hard not to see a settled resentment in every glance, every action. It's as much as I can do to heave myself into the pulpit each week and preach. At least then I have the safety of the pulpit between me and them.

Me and them. That's how it feels right now. I haven't forgotten the advice you gave me and it was really very good, but how can I visit their homes comfortably and share my heart, and theirs with me? How can I open up to them when I'm afraid of them? How can I mix easily with the youth group, when I know they'll have such little respect for my bumbling efforts? Sure, there are people who would love to talk. Harold Carmichael still pesters me to come round to 'share what's on my heart'. I'm really not sure if I want to hear what's on his heart just at this moment. I'd rather hide, and hope they all go away.

You know, I'm just not sure how much longer I can go on.

Yours, in the depths,

Dan

Uncle Eldon

From: eldon@charis.net
Sent: Sunday 19 January, 2:14 p.m.
To: daniel@hubris.com
Subject: Re: Oppression

Dan:

The pain that you feel is very apparent in your latest email. Don't let anyone talk you out of it; it is real and it hurts. Understanding that is crucial if you are to embrace the pain as a part of growth in your personal life and especially your ministry. If you walk away from the pain or internalize it with the hope it will go away, little of good will result.

A key thing is where you say that church is no longer the refuge it once was. You are right in one sense because you are no longer in the church but you are the church, at least in some people's minds. (You can't criticize or complain to a building with much result, but a live person who leads from the building makes a pretty good target.)

The lesson I think before you is how to engage in the life of the church and how to detach from the life of the church, and if that is so, we should talk about boundaries. As I get older I am finding boundaries are being established for me by the doctor and the government and other good people who have my health and welfare at heart. But young men like you will find great advantage in establishing your own boundaries in all areas of your life, for your well-being and also the good of those around you. Especially in ministry. Looking back on some old notes from my early days in ministry, here's what I found. Most of it is advice from older men, but it sure helped me and I hope it will help you.

In ministry there is little natural rhythm because so much of what we do is reaction to situations rather than following through a detailed day-to-day plan. We must establish a rhythm that reflects our values and priorities, so that we can have some hope of sanity. I started by setting three priorities: first, time for God; second, time for family; and third, time for ministry.

The time for family is the one that is most often neglected. I was pleased to read that you went to the park with the children. Do it again. Take the positive view on having to give up your Sundays and several week nights. It means you can have time off mid-week when there's more space at the park and the golf course and the shopping mall. Don't feel guilty when your people see you with your family relaxing when their family is at work. Create space at mealtimes by turning off the phone. When they want you to hear them now, divert them to a time that fits your schedule.

When it is time for ministry you have some advantage over others in that what you get paid to do also takes care of part of your time for God. In ministry my priorities that I pretty much held to were in this order:

1. Personal time with the Lord in prayer and meditation
2. Time in the Word preparing to preach
3. Time in prayer for the people in the church
4. Time for care and compassion for people in the church
5. Time for administration and meetings

Put your mind to it and I think you will find a structure can be created that will allow you better control over your life and still make you available to the people you serve.

The other thing that I think you need desperately, and it is something we in church leadership neglect so freely, is friends and relationships outside the church. You need to have someone to talk with about things other than the church, God, or nuances of theology. It's okay, in fact it's necessary to have an interest in sport, or literature, or the arts, or travel, or anything that is wholesome and recreational. By the way, I encourage you to develop friendships with people who are not Christians, not so you can hit them over the head with your Bible so to speak, but simply for mutual friendship, growth, and encouragement. In today's world it is clear that reconciliation with God is coming primarily through relationship with God's people, and if His part is reconciliation, our part is building relationships.

So right now I think your first priority is to establish boundaries, priorities, and the development of community friendships. They may not take away all the pain but I am confident they will bring greater perspective to your situation and lessen the feeling that your life is in the control of other people.

Share this with Hayley and allow her to steer you as you take care of your body, your emotions, and your soul. Ah, soul. There's a good word to ponder. Is it well with your soul? Know that I am praying to that end for you, and for myself.

I thank God for you every time you come to mind.

Eldon

Daniel Donford

From: daniel@hubris.com
Sent: Monday 17 February, 2:35 a.m.
To: eldon@charis.net
Subject: I Quit!

Dear Uncle Eldon,

Thanks for your last email. I can see what you mean about boundaries. Putting those in place might have made a big difference to my experience here, but it's too late now. I'm drawing the biggest boundary of them all – I'm leaving the ministry. After the worst day of my entire life I have spent the last, few sleepless hours turning it over, and that's what I've decided. Hayley's okay with it, but she says I have to talk it through with you before I mention it to anyone else. So here I am.

You wouldn't believe it. The day started in stormy fashion, literally, and that was just the beginning. Huge angry clouds dumped a massive flood of water that reached almost to the church doorstep, and the accompanying gale nearly swept one section of the roof away. If only it had. We might all have been distracted from the other storm that followed.

Anyway, I preached the worst sermon ever. I doubt if anyone has ever delivered a worse message in the whole history of preaching. I mixed up my words. I had these impossibly long mental blocks. And, honestly, I just don't know if I really believed what I was saying. I'm not sure what I was saying. I didn't want to turn up and hear me, so why would anyone else? It was embarrassing. Preaching is the only thing that I've been able to do over the last few weeks, and now that has deserted me as well.

As always, I tried to make a hasty exit. I should just build a trapdoor behind the pulpit to swallow me up. But Harold Carmichael grabbed me on the way out. He was determined to let me know 'how things are'. He held on to my arm, which was almost more than I could take, and wouldn't let me go until I agreed to a meeting. So I've got that to look forward to later today. Perhaps I'll give him a call and say I'm dead.

And then, as if that wasn't enough of a dismal experience, Doris Blackmore was waiting for me in the foyer like some professional stalker. She didn't say a word. She just gave me this glare that chilled me inside and out. She looked so angry at me. And – this is the hard part – I was angry back. I stormed over and practically yelled at her. I let her know how it felt to wear her hostility week after week. I told her how the rejection I experienced from every single person in this church was personified in her. All my frustration and anger and disorientation and hurt got dumped on her in one go, just like that storm. I'm sure it reached her doorstep – she was crying by the end of it, and so was I. When I turned around there was the whole church watching, listening. They couldn't have missed a word. They stood there, unmoving, for one endless awful moment. Then Frank Schumacher sniffed his disdain, dismissed me with a glance and walked through the crowd with his back turned towards me. Well, fine. Let him go. I'm out of here.

So I raced out the door and headed for home, and I wrestled with it all through the day. I was so angry to start with, and then empty, and then ashamed. I should never have yelled at Doris Blackmore like that. Part of me still relishes every word that I said, and that just makes me even more ashamed. No pastor should behave like that. I'm appalled and embarrassed, even now. I think it would be better for everyone concerned if I wasn't here. I'm not cut out for this pastoring business. I'm a failure, a disaster. Things are worse now than when I came. So much for Sydney Schneider's neat and tidy templates. So much for church growth in four easy steps. There's nothing easy about this, nothing; and I'm not up to it.

I feel scared for the future. I don't know what I'll do or how we'll support ourselves. All my friends will think I'm a failure. The church will write me off. And I've let you down. But I can't see any other way out. In just seven months all I've done is make a mess of things. If God wants to turn this place around, he'll have to find someone else to do it. It's over. I've finished. We're through. I quit.

Maybe now I can get some sleep.

Dan

Harry Compton

From: hjcompton@compton.com
Sent: Monday 17 February, 6:57 a.m.
To: murkowskis@griblet.org
Subject: Make a Move!

Tony

When are you moving? This guy's a dead loss. He's finished. Yesterday he practically screamed at Doris Blackmore in front of everyone just after the service finished. He can't lead. He can't preach. He can't cope.

It's time we had someone who can. I will do whatever you need, just get here soon.

Harry

Uncle Eldon

From:	eldon@charis.net
Sent:	Monday 17 February, 11:48 a.m.
To:	daniel@hubris.com
Subject:	Re: I Quit!

Dan:

You have certainly made your point clear when you say you quit and you are through. I'm not surprised. As I look back over my ministry life I can't count the times I've used those very words, sometimes out loud.

There is no question it was a stormy day at the church. There is no question you feel inadequate for the task, no question from your responses of frustration and anger that you are hurting to the core, and certainly no question you married a smart woman when she tells you to keep quiet about your planned resignation for a time.

I believe it was Socrates who said that the 'unexamined life is not worth living'. So where shall we start? I suggest you begin by getting some good rest, a time where you occupy your mind and body so intensely on something other than the church that some renewal of sanity ensues.

After that you may be more of a mind to consider these thoughts I write. There are two Scripture portions I want you to look over and consider.

The first is in Galatians where Paul says to the people 'You were running well, who stopped you?' As a man in your early thirties, a young man, the temptation to give up is strong. You have lived long enough to be conscious of a past, and I notice men of your age are often tempted to bury ambitions, even ideals, and stop short of their full potential. That would be a pity in your case. Your age could be more correctly described as a phase, the end of preparation and the beginning of realization. Right now the realization is brutal in its application but I encourage you to make friends with life. Deep in your heart you know you are in the right place.

The second Scripture is 2 Corinthians 4:16-18. It's a passage that will help you position yourself to focus on the right things. The three verses simply encourage you to move your focus from suffering and sin to inward renewal, from your troubles to the eternal glory, and from what is seen to include also things that are unseen, that is, what God sees.

This is what I meant earlier when I said you are in the phase of realization. Repositioning, refocusing, will help you realize there is another point of view on any current situation. You don't have to stay as you are. You shouldn't want to stay as you are. God is not encumbered with what you feel right now. He sees and plans a bright future for you, not ignoring present feelings but using them as a springboard for growth towards greater maturity as you trust in Him. Inward renewal, eternal glory, are attractive and achievable.

One more thing. One day you may have the great joy and privilege of taking your daughter by the arm and walking her down the aisle to meet her bridegroom. I've done it twice and let me tell you it is about as emotional a day as you can have. But you don't have to wait. Every day you have the privilege and joy of preparing your people to be the bride of Christ. It is as if you have them by the arm and you are walking them down the aisle. The bridegroom awaits and you are charged with making them as ready as possible for that great day. It sounds like you have a big job on your hands, but you can do it. With the power that God provides you can join the apostle and have confidence that one day you will present all of them 'perfect in Christ'.

Think about it.

Eldon

Daniel Donford

From:	daniel@hubris.com
Sent:	Friday 21 February, 11:40 a.m.
To:	eldon@charis.net
Subject:	I Don't Quit

Dear Uncle Eldon,

What a week!! After such a woeful beginning it became the most wonderful, encouraging few days I've had in a long time. It was so unexpected, so jarring, that it is nothing short of a resurrection. Somehow, I have come alive with it.

I don't know what to begin with, so I'll cover it all in the order it happened. I think I told you that, with threat of force, Harold Carmichael had pinned me down to an appointment. I was ready to run, but Hayley made me keep it. Looking back now, I can't believe how badly I misjudged that wonderful man. I'm not sure what it was – I think his glass eye unnerved me. And I must admit I dismissed him because he's so old, at least as old as Frank – and I guess I lumped them together in the same casket. Anyway, Harold was so encouraging. Sure, his ideas are quaint and unrealistic, but at least he had some. He wants to see this place change as much as I do. He even gave me a wink when our discussion came around to Frank, as if he wants me to keep battling. In fact – and I still can't quite believe this – he says the whole church is quietly cheering me on. Well, they sure don't look like they are! But he explained that they've been through eight pastors and they're hurt and they expect me to move on like the rest of them so they're slow to open up and give me their trust. But underneath all that, they are desperately hoping I can pull this off. Can you believe it!

Then, on Tuesday afternoon, Hayley and I had a visit from Alice, the youth group girl I mentioned a while back – the one who asked me to talk about the glories of Christ. It turns out she was serious! There she was sitting in my office – this shy, hesitant young woman – and she told us how I had inspired her in the middle of that dreadful meeting by dropping everything and talking about the Lord. She wondered why she didn't have the same passion and she wanted me to share it with her again. Not only that, after we talked for a while she realized that she'd never arrived at a faith of her own. And there, kneeling on the floor of my office, she and Hayley prayed together. They were both crying at the end of it. I was exhilarated. I had no idea that God could work through such a broken, pitiful creature as me, but he did.

I resolved at that point to head around to see Doris Blackmore to apologize. I didn't wait, I just went. When she saw me she burst into tears. I thought I'd done the wrong thing again, but after a while it all came out. She admitted that she's been having an affair for these last two years with a man at her work. She's been feeling increasingly guilty, and my preaching seemed to provoke her conscience every single week. So she wasn't angry at me at all. Well, she kind of was. Like you said – I'm the visible face of the church, and God, and her conscience, I guess. She readily forgave me for my outburst on Sunday, with such understanding! She showed me a side of her I would never have guessed. I offered to stay with her while she confessed to Andrew, or to send Hayley around as moral support, but she chose to approach him on her own. I'm not too sure what his response was, but it's a good sign that they have started some counseling to work it all through. I guess that's only the beginning, and who knows how it will end, but it seems an encouraging first step through deep waters.

Even that's not all. Yesterday morning I was reading my Bible when some verses got my pulse racing. I've been planning to read through Jeremiah – feeling a bit like a weeping prophet myself – when I read this in the first chapter: 'Before I formed you in the womb I knew you, before you were born I set you apart; I appointed you as a prophet to the nations'. Those three words, 'I appointed you', hammered at my heart, as if God had reserved them just for me. Jeremiah then objects that he's too young (I know how he felt) but God wasn't having any of it. I felt that too. It's strange, but I sensed a very clear call. I know that I'm in the right place. I know God wants me here, as hard as it is and as feeble as I am. There's been no mistake. I'm in the right place and your latest message simply confirmed it for me. You were right not to let me off the hook (just like Jeremiah). It was so encouraging to learn that I'm not alone. Others have been here before me, Hayley's here with me, Harold is backing me, you are at my side, and God has brought me here for a purpose. My resignation is duly retracted. I'm pleased now that I never mentioned it to anyone else. On Sunday I'll apologize to the whole church for my behaviour last Sunday. Then I know we can move on to better times. I can't help feeling that we've all turned some sort of corner.

Thanks for your navigation.

Dan

Daniel Donford

From:	daniel@hubris.com
Sent:	Sunday 23 February, 1:13 p.m.
To:	eldon@charis.net
Subject:	The Apology

Dear Uncle Eldon,

I thought I'd send you a quick email to say that it's been a very good day. I really am in a very different place from where I was a week ago. This morning I publicly apologized to Doris Blackmore and then I apologized to the whole church. I felt like I had nothing to lose, so I tried to be as honest as I could about my failings and asked for their patience and forgiveness. I think that's what I got from them. Hayley said I did okay. I went home wonderfully encouraged.

You'll hardly believe one other reason for that: Meredith Bellweather has joined the church. She turned up today out of the blue, explaining that she has decided to leave her present community of worship (it took me three minutes to work out she was talking about her cats) and to join a regular congregation. It turns out that she really appreciated my visit to her home and my warmth and enthusiasm that day she met me in the supermarket. She said to me, 'Don, you are such a godly young man – if this is the church you're in, I want to be in it too', and that was that. She sat right next to Harry with not a gap between them, looking up at him often, smiling and making comments. Did he look happy about it? No he did not, no indeed. I think his practical joke has backfired badly. It's an unusual form of encouragement but I'll take it. Whatever condition I am in at the moment, I'm not beaten yet.

So I think the business of my outburst last Sunday is all behind me.

Dan

Martha Krinks

From:	martha_krinks@endora.com
Sent:	Monday 24 February, 10:03 a.m.
To:	jdandemtrout@vmail.org
Subject:	Sunday

My dear Janice,

Thank you so much for the very nice sweater that you knitted for Stafford. He looks positively regal in it. I do not know how you get the elbows to sit just as nicely as you do but it really looks good on him. It was such a wonderful delight to open up your package and find it inside. You are really so thoughtful.

Yes, I am pleased to say that dear Daniel seems to be doing a whole lot better though I had to wonder about that this time last week. You would not believe it. The poor man. I do not know quite what got into him. It all happened last Sunday (not yesterday but the one before). Just after the service finished I was chatting away when I heard raised voices coming from the foyer. I hurried out to see what was going on and who do you suppose was doing all that yelling? It was Daniel! My heart sank. I just could not believe my eyes and ears. I still do not know quite what he had to get off his chest but once he finished he turned around to see us all staring. His face went so red and then it went white and then he stormed off out the door and into the rain without even so much as a jacket to keep him dry.

Well. You can imagine how people talked about him after that. They could not talk about anything else. I did my best to calm things down and reassure people but really there was very little I could say. On the way home Stafford wondered if it was time to form another search committee. He just could not see how poor young Daniel could carry on.

But yesterday things were so very different. Daniel told us about how much he had changed in the last week. He began by publicly apologizing for yelling at dear Doris. It was such a lovely moment. Doris was there to hear it and though we could hardly hear what she was saying for all her tears and sniffles it was clear that she was willing to forgive Daniel for everything he had said and done. And then Daniel apologized to us as well for setting such a poor example. You know for the first time I think he just let himself be himself. I don't recall I have ever seen him quite so unguarded. The conceit that others complain about just fell away and he was really quite sweet and endearing. He told us about this lovely young girl called Alice who came to faith right there in his office and he was just so encouraged. And then he told us about the blessing of some verses in Jeremiah (I think they were from chapter 1) and he preached from those in his sermon and I dare say it was one of the most encouraging and inspiring talks we have heard in years. I've always said that Daniel is a wonderful preacher but he really came alive yesterday and I do think he lifted us all up at the same time. I doubt that everyone has been entirely forgiving but I am pretty sure that, having seen Daniel at his very worst and at his very best we'll stick with him a while longer. Who knows? He could turn out to be a fine pastor after all.

Well dear, I am supposed to be babysitting for my neighbour, Mary-Ann this morning (she's the one with the twins) so I'd better head on over.

Give my love to Ed.

Martha

Sam Campbell

From:	samcampbell368@icarus.com
Sent:	Wednesday 12 March, 8:17 a.m.
To:	daniel@hubris.com
Subject:	Good to meet you

Hey Dan.

It was great to meet you yesterday at the pastors' conference and to hear how things are going over at Broadfield. I can still remember what it was like when I started out in ministry. I still feel like I'm starting out in ministry – ha ha. You seem to be doing really well. You may not feel like it, I know. But you've been through a pretty tough time and you seem to have survived okay. You should be encouraged.

I thought that we clicked pretty well and I've been wondering if you and I can maybe keep in touch. You know, send emails and meet up from time to time? We might even do that on a regular basis. Coffee once a month perhaps? Just a thought. But I know I could do with the fellowship. Even after all this time I still haven't got someone outside of the church I can confide in. I haven't even got anyone inside the church. ☺ Over the last few months I've been thinking that I need to find a person I can be honest with.

I hope this isn't coming on too heavy for you. Just say if you think I'm asking too much. You may not have the same sort of need for this as I do because you have your uncle Alvin to call on. I only wish I had someone like him in my life. I think it would make a big difference. But if you would like to get together now and then, I'd be mighty appreciative. What do you think?

Sam

Daniel Donford

From:	daniel@hubris.com
Sent:	Wednesday 12 March, 10:43 a.m.
To:	samcampbell368@icarus.com
Subject:	Re: Good to meet you

Dear Sam,

I was really excited to get your message – thanks. I'd be very keen to catch up with you once a month (and we can keep in touch more often if we need to, with phone calls and emails). We could meet up halfway between us in one of the suburbs. How about Greenacres? There's a café there on the main street called Oak Tree Coffee and Cake. Hayley and I discovered it a while ago on our way across town. Would that suit you?

I know what you mean about having my Uncle Eldon (not 'Alvin', but close). He is amazing. It's so reassuring knowing that I have his experience and wisdom to call on when I need it. But it makes me think that I need more of that kind of input, not less. I definitely see the value of it. Like you, I haven't yet found anyone around town that I can open up to. And I really enjoyed our conversation yesterday. So count me in.

I'm free next Tuesday and Thursday afternoons. What time suits you?

Dan

Sam Campbell

From:	samcampbell368@icarus.com
Sent:	Wednesday 12 March, 10:44 a.m.
To:	daniel@hubris.com
Subject:	Re: Good to meet you

Hey Dan.

Thanks for your reply. Thanks for welcoming my idea. This is going to be cool. I'll see you at Oak Tree next Tuesday at 2:00? Okay?

Sam

Daniel Donford

From:	daniel@hubris.com
Sent:	Thursday 3 April, 10:01 a.m.
To:	eldon@charis.net
Subject:	Visitation

Dear Uncle Eldon,

My pastoral visitation has been going okay lately, to the point where I'm even beginning to look forward to it (well, not always). I've been careful to follow your advice, which I'm sure has made the difference. But something happened yesterday that I thought I'd tell you about. I think you'll enjoy it. I can't say that I enjoyed it, but I am beginning to see the funny side.

Emily has persisted in her campaign for us to buy a cat. Things had escalated to the point where I thought drastic action was required, so I decided to take her on one of my visits to see Meredith Bellweather. That way Emily would be deterred by seeing these awful creatures in such potent numbers. I don't know what I was thinking. I should have realized that it was never going to work. I suspect Hayley knew alright. She gave me one of her shrewd, knowing smiles as we left the house (when will I learn to pay attention to those!). She and Emily are in the same camp on this issue, and I suppose David, being a mere three years old, is as well. I can consider myself badly outnumbered.

A visit to Meredith would fix that, I thought, but I was playing right into their hands, wasn't I? So there we all were. I may as well not have been in the room. The two of them spent the whole time caught up in the cats –

meeting them, counting them, feeding them, stroking them (that's when they weren't admiring Emily's golden curls or talking about dresses). Any attempt of mine to bring the conversation around to anything halfway meaningful was met with utter defeat. And so I trudged out of there precisely two hours later to ponder the full extent of my setback. There was only one brief moment of illusory hope. Just when we got to the car, Emily said, 'I don't want a cat anymore', to my giddy relief. 'I want eighteen cats – just like Miss Bellweather.'

I don't suppose you've got any advice for warding off cats. I'm not sure how much longer I can hold out.

On a more promising note, I've struck up a new friendship with a pastor across town. His name is Sam Campbell. He's a little older than I am, with three kids, and he's been in the ministry for almost eight years. His church is a long way ahead of ours and doing well. I really like him, and he's good to talk to. We've agreed to meet every month for coffee. That should help relieve the isolation I've been feeling, don't you think?

Dan

Daniel Donford

From:	daniel@hubris.com
Sent:	Wednesday 16 April, 7:43 p.m.
To:	eldon@charis.net
Subject:	Funerals

Dear Uncle Eldon,

You can learn a lot about someone from their funeral. That's what I decided today, when I went to Frank Schumacher's. That's right, Frank passed away on Sunday afternoon. He had some chest pains about half-past-two, and within a few minutes he was gone.

So today I went to his funeral, me and very few others. I was struck by how small his life was in the end. Now I can't understand how he held us in his thrall for so long. I came away feeling strangely sad, not for the usual reason that you're sad at funerals. (I can't honestly say that I will miss the man. In fact, I've woken up the last few mornings relieved, even elated, that I don't have to face the problems he represented.) No, I was sad because I caught a glimpse of his life as it really was. And you were right. I think he was a lonely, troubled old man. Actually, he wasn't that old. It turns out he was only 73, so how did he come to seem so old? That's sad as well.

The most glaring fact was how few of us were there today. His six children were back, of course, but I'd never noticed that all but one had moved away from town. Some of them live at the other end of the country. It's like they couldn't bear to stay around him. Certainly they shed no tears for him this afternoon. They seemed more concerned to comfort Carmel, Frank's wife, who looked bereft and confused. She's always reminded me of a tender flower that's been crushed and bruised. She might have bounced back once, but it's probably been too long. I don't know what she'll do now.

So there was hardly anyone else. I was surprised by how few people in the church came to the service. Harold Carmichael was there, and we sat together. It's hard to believe but he actually cracked a few jokes during the eulogy. He surprises me some more every time I see him. He was quite funny and I had to stop myself from laughing.

So there were moments of relief from the sadness of it all. I discovered that Frank was something of a visionary in his time. He was the one who had the youth hall extended to develop the children's ministry. It seems sad and ironic that he could not allow in his final years what he himself had done as a young man. What changed? Where did the vision go, the passion? When did conviction give way to control? I guess I'll never know, but it was a sobering lesson. I made a promise to myself not to end up like Frank, and to let go of things when it's time for others to be set free.

You know, it's sad. The last thing Frank said to me on Sunday was 'No'. That's what I'll remember him for, that final word. I'll look back and see him as one big No. I wonder if they'll put that solitary adjective on his tombstone: a huge 'No' engraved in granite. That was Frank, at least as I'll remember him. Very sad.

Dan

Uncle Eldon

From: eldon@charis.net
Sent: Thursday 17 April, 9:17 a.m.
To: daniel@hubris.com
Subject: Re: Funerals

Dan:

I am sorry to learn of Frank's death. I never knew the man, yet from your descriptions I feel I know much about him. It is sad when a man passes away and there is a sense that his legacy is not altogether positive. I wonder if a part of your sadness is that you nursed a hope to influence him towards positive attitudes and the openness to change that apparently marked his earlier life. Now that possibility has gone.

At my stage of life I keep asking the question: 'How can I finish well?' The older I get, the more convinced I become that the way we finish our lives is determined very early in adult life. It's the old illustration about the tree trunk that is pliable and able to be straightened in the early years but impossible to adjust in maturity. Particularly in men I see the need in the younger years to have goals and the energy and opportunity to achieve things, if we are to grow towards maturity. But as time goes by that need changes into a need to rest in what God has achieved, so that we can model Christian maturity out of wholeness.

For many an older man, the wounds of life (which I now realize are almost inevitable) have not been allowed to do the work of deepening the soul. Instead, energy has been focused on blaming and complaining. That leads to withdrawal from anything to do with sacrificial service and the modeling of servanthood, and to isolation from those he could be encouraging and who could encourage him. This is the saddest ending I can imagine, because the last word from his lips, like Frank's last word to you, is 'No'.

Dan, say yes to God every time. Say no to bitterness and anger always. Choose now, while you are young.

Share your dreams with the Pastor across town who is a little further on the journey than you, encourage him to say yes to God, and agree that together you will finish well.

Finally, give thanks to the Lord for the life of Frank, for the things God did through him that will last for eternity, and for the lessons you learned from his life that spur you towards a closer walk with God.

You are a great encouragement to me. Thank you for taking the time to share your journey with me. Always, you are in my prayers.

Eldon

Harry Compton

From: hjcompton@compton.com
Sent: Friday 25 April, 3:15 p.m.
To: murkowskis@griblet.org
Subject: Re: Plans

Tony

Good. I've been telling you to do something for months now. I still think your best chance was the Doris Blackmore episode. But we didn't move quickly enough and Dan made a much better recovery than I gave him credit for.

But he's still a lost cause, especially now that Frank's out of the way. So it's a good moment to edge back in. See you soon.

Harry

Sam Campbell

From:	samcampbell368@icarus.com
Sent:	Thursday 1 May, 10:00 a.m.
To:	daniel@hubris.com
Subject:	Meeting

Hey Dan.

Thanks for fitting me in yesterday. I know how busy you are. Yet you gave up some time for me just when I needed it. I won't forget that.

Hey, it really helped to talk things through with you ahead of the meeting last night. It went better than I had expected. I still think that it was a mistake to bring Mervin into the Eldership so quickly. We should have taken the time to get to know him a little better, or at least I should have. I think I told you he has been in the church for about eighteen months. But it's actually less than that, maybe just over a year. I'm also not sure exactly how his name came up for nomination in the first place. But that's all in the past now and I can see no way of correcting my mistake except at great cost, because he seems to have gained the confidence of the other Elders. I'd also forgotten that Barbara had a bad feeling about him. I should have learned years ago to pay attention to the intuition of my wife. I guess that's another lesson learned all over again, and far too late. I hope this is at least of some use to you – don't repeat my mistakes!

But the meeting went okay. Mervin explained to everyone basically what I said to you, that he wanted me to show a more aggressive leadership style. I don't think he used exactly that word but as far as I can tell that's what he means. He wants a clearer vision and direction from the front. I tried to explain that it's not really my style. He pounced on me when I used the words 'laid back' and said that the church was nothing to be laid back about. I think he went too far with that comment and a couple of the others challenged him on it. They said that they appreciated my gentle leadership style. But they also suggested that I give some thought to what Mervin is saying and I agreed to do that. So I'm not too sure if I'm better or worse off than I was before the meeting, but at least there was some support. Between you and me, I'm feeling a little bit vulnerable. Hopefully Mervin will be satisfied with that, but part of me worries that it's really only the beginning.

So thanks again for helping me to think it all through. I am very grateful to you. If you don't mind I might give you a call sometime on Sunday afternoon to catch up again. I'm preaching on John 15 this week – 'abide in me'. I'm trying to figure out what that means, especially at a time like this.

Sam

Daniel Donford

From:	daniel@hubris.com
Sent:	Thursday 1 May, 3:11 p.m.
To:	samcampbell368@icarus.com
Subject:	Re: Meeting

Dear Sam,

You really don't need to thank me for meeting up with you yesterday. I was only too happy to be there for you. I know that in a similar circumstance (and let's face it, that's bound to happen) you'd be there for me too. So ask anytime you need me. We're here for each other.

This is just a thought, but would you and Barbara like to come over for dinner on Sunday? I know it's crazy to do this in the middle of winter but we've just bought a new grill that we'd like to try out on you. If you came around 4:00pm that would give us time to talk while our two play with your girls. What do you think?

Dan

Daniel Donford

From:	daniel@hubris.com
Sent:	Thursday 1 May, 3:13 p.m.
To:	eldon@charis.net
Subject:	Nominating Elders

Dear Uncle Eldon,

A quick question that comes to mind: what is the best way for appointing new Elders? It's not that we'll be doing that anytime soon but it's also never too early to start thinking about it so I don't make any costly mistakes.

Dan

Uncle Eldon

From: eldon@charis.net
Sent: Saturday 3 May, 2:37 p.m.
To: daniel@hubris.com
Subject: Re: Nominating Elders

Dan:

You're right. It's never too early to be thinking about things likely to come up soon, and identifying and training Elders is certainly going to be one of them. In fact, now could be the right time for you to be doing just that. Frank has passed on, Stafford seems to have a new enthusiasm for the role, and I would guess that Carlton is not lacking in commitment to you and to the church. A new chapter can begin as you draw into Eldership those who meet the scriptural qualifications and who can bring fresh insights to encourage, support and even at times challenge your direction.

There are two lessons in particular that I want to pass on to you. I learned them a long time ago, the hard way. But they also represent wisdom given to me by older leaders who had my best interests at heart and who helped me to avoid my previous missteps.

This is the first: 'Be very slow to offer a ministry to someone who seems unable to live without it'.

I wish I had done that every time, but fighting against that resolve is the ongoing struggle to find willing people to be involved in various ministries. It feels so good when someone offers enthusiastically to do something, and the natural response is to sign them on. But ministry is primarily a work of the heart. What joy it is to find that a person's offer to serve is the result of submission to Christ following significant prayer, meditation, and consultation with close confidants. When that happens, say yes. Conversely, how hard it is to address the heart issues with one whose identity is tied to what they do, who wants to control and to have a title apparently more significant to them than 'servant of Christ'. Good people with wrong motives are not in a posture to draw God's blessing, and without the blessing of God not much of worth will be accomplished. Be strong in being very slow to offer ministry to someone who cannot live without it, especially when that ministry is Eldership.

And the second lesson is this: 'Before appointing an Elder, make sure he understands that any authority that might be attached to the role is given that he might serve, not given that he might set himself apart.'

If he needs the title, it probably won't be a good experience; if he understands and embraces the role, keep moving forward. Shepherds are on the same level as the sheep: sometimes in front; other times behind; but always among them, in the sense they are close enough to notice a limp, hear a cry, or smell sickness. I would think there are already some in your church who are operating just like that but without the title. Maybe they could be approached for input as to who they would see as additional Elders, creating an opportunity for them to be asked about their own interest.

I was never a fan of asking the congregation for nominations or involving them in a vote to choose some and reject others, although I appreciate that is the governance structure of many churches. My preferred method was to invite the existing and previous Elders plus a few mature, godly men and women to recommend 2-3 names. In a congregation the size of yours, Dan, I would think you will not get more than 4-5 different names and you would certainly have a couple of names that are on everyone's list. Then the existing Elders would start a process of scrutiny and prayer.

One of the key things as we got close to agreement was what I call 'chemistry' between the candidate and the existing Elders. Elders develop a close bond in ministry and they are called to deal with difficult issues involving people and their relationship with God. It is imperative that the Elders hold one another accountable to a deep, transparent, spiritual walk; that they operate as a team; and that they model Christ-like, grace-filled relationships in the group. I think this has some similarities to the marriage relationship, and so, as we worked through candidates for Eldership (and for additional pastoral staff), I would often use the phrase 'better to be single than married to the wrong person'.

I understand that you and others will have different points of view on this subject and I have seen many methods result in many fine Elder groups in churches I have observed, but I pass on my experience for reference as you do this for the first time in your ministry.

One day you will look back over your ministry and give thanks to God for the close, enduring friendships developed with your Elders, as I do now. Those bonds were formed as we served together: encouraging, confronting, laughing, crying, praying, trusting, asking forgiveness. I would trust them with my life. And so will you.

God bless you Pastor,

Eldon

Sam Campbell

From: samcampbell368@icarus.com
Sent: Sunday 4 May, 9:46 p.m.
To: daniel@hubris.com
Subject: Re: Meeting

Hey Dan.

We've just arrived home and put the girls to bed. On the way back Barbara and I were talking about how much we appreciated the evening with you and Hayley. We love you both and look forward to spending more time with you. Thanks for helping us through this tough patch. When we got home there was a message from Mervin on our answerphone asking to meet with me again. That would have been even more deflating if we didn't have you guys around to encourage us. So thanks!

Sam

(See you for coffee next Tuesday. Can we make it 3:00 this time?)

Daniel Donford

From:	daniel@hubris.com
Sent:	Thursday 8 May, 2:59 p.m.
To:	eldon@charis.net
Subject:	Coping With Criticism

Dear Uncle Eldon,

Do you remember me saying that I was meeting regularly with a pastor from across town, Sam Campbell? It's been going really well the few times we've met up for coffee. Last weekend we had Sam, his wife Barbara and their three girls over for dinner. They're a lovely family. We like them a lot and it's great to have someone who is ahead in the game from where I am. His church is probably about twice as big as ours and it seems to be in good shape. I haven't yet been over to visit it but I'd like to one Sunday. I hear good things, and not just from Sam.

He's an interesting guy. For a start, he's very tall and very thin. He must be a good four inches taller than I am. Needless to say he'd make a great basketball player and I think he used to play at college, but I get the feeling he's never had the passion you need to compete at the top level. He may be tall but he's also gentle with it, and there is something almost reluctant or reticent about him, as if he doesn't quite have the self-confidence to give himself fully to his talents and strengths. I'm not sure how that plays out in his ministry because he seems to be doing very well in it. Then again, for all the height advantage he has over the rest of us, he sometimes seems, I don't know, as if he's daunted by other people. He walks with a kind of stoop, as if he's embarrassed about his height and wants to minimize it. I try to encourage him but it does seem a little depressing that he's several years ahead in ministry and dealing with people is still proving to be about as challenging for him as it is for me. I keep that thought to myself, because he seems to appreciate our conversations together.

Mind you, all that may be just the season he's in at the moment, which is not a particularly happy one. I said things are going well in his church, and generally they are, but lately he's been getting a hard time. One of his new Elders is critical of Sam's leadership style and says he needs to be more assertive and directive. This new guy (his name is Mervin) was the CEO of quite a large company. About eighteen months ago he took early retirement. I guess he thinks he can transfer that kind of leadership into the church. And apparently others are beginning to agree with him.

I think Sam is finding it pretty tough and is not sure how to deal with these attacks (that's what they feel like to him). I'm meeting him for coffee again on Tuesday but I wondered if you have any advice I can pass on to him? It will be useful for me too because there does seem to be plenty of scope to find myself criticized as well. I guess that's true of all pastors?

As always, thanks for your wisdom, patience and availability.

Dan

Uncle Eldon

From:	eldon@charis.net
Sent:	Monday 12 May, 11:42 a.m.
To:	daniel@hubris.com
Subject:	Re: Coping With Criticism

Dan,

I loved your email, not because your buddy is under fire from one of his elders, but because he has a friend across town who is there for him.

That's you, and you are showing yourself as a man with a pastoral heart who is moving his concerns away from self and embracing the pain of a fellow Pastor. The apostle wrote about you when he exhorted us to 'bear one another's burdens and thus fulfil the law of Christ'. And we used to sing about you as youth (usually around a campfire): 'we are pilgrims on a journey, we are brothers on the road, we are here to help each other walk the mile and bear the load.' I am so encouraged to see that in you.

But your friend Sam is not encouraged as you are, saying that one of his Elders doesn't like his leadership style.

Criticism penetrates to find the ego, and sometimes does not have to dig very deep. We can say that Christ is our sufficiency, that we are 'hid with Christ in God' and that 'we have been crucified with Christ', but the words they say hurt. And as Scripture tells us that 'the wounds of friends are faithful', we think that these words must be from enemies because they sure don't sound faithful.

So you and Sam pray first and then I would suggest you turn in Scripture to Moses. Stephen's testimony in Acts 7 tells us that 'Moses was no ordinary child. He was educated in all the wisdom of Egypt and was powerful in speech and action.' That certainly sets him apart from most, but I am not convinced that his success came from traditional learning. So many times in the journey of the Israelites across the wilderness we read that the people complained to Moses, and Moses asked the Lord. A part of me thinks that the people were really complaining to God but were frightened to speak to him directly so they went through their leader. And criticism feels better when we can see the person who is upsetting us as we tell him what we think of his leadership. I would say Moses is a self-confident, even angry man at the beginning, but in the hands of God for 40 years of wilderness training he becomes submissive to God and His plan. He throws the symbol of the only authority he has, his shepherd's staff, on the ground and sees its potential danger as a snake. Then God gives it back as a staff, not the staff of Moses any more, but as he loads his donkey to return to confront the Pharaoh, we read that he included 'the staff of God'. The life of Moses has given way to the life of God.

No wonder we remember him as a great leader: he carries the staff of God and sees plagues come upon the enemy, the Red Sea part, water from the rock, victory over the Amalekites, and much more. He still is human and makes mistakes, but Moses stands out to me as the man who listened to all the criticism and then saw it as God's issue and almost always refused to take it on himself.

I hope you and Sam are doing better in this than I did, Dan, because as easy as it sounds, I failed many times, in so many ways. We do have to listen, we do have to try to understand the complainant's perspective, we do have to search our hearts to ensure we are not violating God's standards, and we do have to consider the source of the criticism. But we don't have to compromise to please others, and we don't have to look for people's affirmation as our source of worth or fulfilment. In the end, some criticisms are not worth heeding.

Because Sam's issue involves an Elder, I would strongly suggest he talk to one of the longer-serving Elders, advising him of what has happened and asking for his intervention. Sam may want to ask that Elder to call for Mervin (who I see is new to the group) to bring his complaint to the full Elders' meeting in writing. Then it can be determined by the whole leadership if Sam is delinquent in any area of his agreed-to job description in terms of method, or if he is violating any biblical principle. If the answer is yes, Sam needs to change; if no, Mervin needs to withdraw his complaint and agree to address future concerns through the Elder group. The process to achieve this is best done by the Elders as a whole rather than by Sam on his own.

The most important thing for Sam is how he reacts to the criticism. Reactions quickly reveal character. And remember that character is the accumulation of habitual behaviour that can become permanent, fixed, and consequential.

I'll be praying for both you and Sam.

Eldon

Daniel Donford

From:	danield@charis.net
Sent:	Sunday 25 May, 2:53 p.m.
To:	eldon@charis.net
Subject:	Church

Dear Uncle Eldon,

You'll never guess what we did at church today. I can hardly believe it myself. We didn't have it! Or we did, but it was different.

Let me explain. It was another stormy day, which brought back some unpleasant memories, let me tell you. There was flooding around the town, on the streets and in some houses. A couple of roads were blocked. And I guess some people decided to stay at home instead of coming to church. So when it came time to start the service, there weren't too many of us there. About fifteen or twenty, I suppose. We were sitting around talking about the weather, and eleven o'clock came and went. Our conversation drifted towards the church, and it was kind of weird. We talked in hushed tones for a while, almost as if we had Frank looking over our shoulder. Perhaps it was having Carmel there that made us nervous, but she said nothing. Who knows what she was thinking?

Anyway, Harry Compton finally said that we'd better get on with the service. He likes everything to be organized and he doesn't cope too well when things don't go to schedule. But no one else wanted to start. We were all too excited talking about the church, and we felt like naughty schoolchildren whose teacher hasn't turned up.

Harold Carmichael pointed out that this was the richest community of the Sunday saints that he'd experienced in a long while, and suggested we keep discussing.

So we did. Harry looked none too pleased, but the rest of us got quite carried away. We tossed around some changes we could make to the programme, which was exciting enough. There were some odd ideas, that's for sure, but it was fun and we thought of some things that would never have occurred to me. At one point Hayley laughed out loud, which got us all going. It was so much fun. I realized then that I had never laughed in church all year, not once. Pretty soon we realized that to change our approach we'd need to change the building. We even debated whether to sell this one and buy something else. Can you imagine! I'm sure Frank was turning in his freshly dug grave (I'm not sure of the theology of that, but you know what I mean). Meanwhile, Carmel sat there quiet and serene.

You know, I was fairly quiet myself through all of this. I think I might at last be learning to keep my mouth shut (although I have been sowing seeds in plenty of other contexts, quiet conversations that may now be bearing fruit). God seemed to be leading the discussion just fine without my involvement. I helped give it a steer now and then, but they hardly needed me. And then a strange thing happened. I began to feel such a love for these people. Just when they were discussing changing the building and taking a new approach with so much enthusiasm and excitement it all seemed so much less important to me than them – their souls, their lives, their growth. I think we all realized today, if we'd forgotten it before, that church is about the people in the end. Not starting a service at a certain time, or doing things a particular way. It's about God's Kingdom, and that means people. I don't know where our ideas will go. I don't know if change will happen as fast as I want it to. But I'm prepared to be patient, to let God set the pace, and to travel alongside even the slowest member if it will help them to get there in the end. Today we all had a special sense that God might be on the move. Most of us, I think, could hardly wait to see what happens next.

Then Harry Compton burst our bubble. He had said nothing all through our discussion. But just at the end he asked us where were we going to get the money for all this. Good question. No one said it out loud, of course, but if Carmel decides to move away we'll lose Frank's financial support along with Frank. Then we'd be scratching around just to make ends meet, let alone contemplate a building project. So thank you Harry! I suppose reality had to sink in, but what an amazing morning. I won't forget that 'service' in a hurry, and I have this hunch that God will come through for us, somehow.

Dan

PS, You'll see from my email address that I've changed my internet service provider. The old one wasn't working too well, so I've changed to the one you use.

Uncle Eldon

From: eldon@charis.net
Sent: Tuesday 27 May, 1:28 p.m.
To: danield@charis.net
Subject: Re: Church

Dan:

I love to hear the excitement for ministry and the church that is coming through your last couple of emails, and have to say that every time I go online these days, I hope to find something from you in the mailbox. Thanks for allowing me to speak into your life, it's something that others did for me when I was younger, and if I can pass anything on that is helpful, I'll thank the Lord.

I love it when the weather or some other situation upsets the regular Sunday routine. As you know, during the winter here we get snow a couple of times a year, and only the hardy or foolhardy get through to the church. The treasurer frets because there is no offering, but the rest of us love to sit in a circle with coffee and snacks. It's one reason why church camps are valuable, because worshipping in a different setting for some reason loosens the tongues and the inhibitions. If it's true that the precursor to vision is discontent with the present (think about that in terms of dreams for your marriage and personal life), then informal situations as you experienced last Sunday allow people to see what a preferred future could look like. God wasn't too concerned that you missed the 11 am start time or that you didn't follow the programme you had prepared, but then God looks at the heart, not the clock. Which leads me to say also that God is not as worried about where the money to fund the vision will come from, as apparently Harry

Compton is. Frank's widow may leave town with her financial support but the church need not worry. It's been my experience in the church that we support financially what we value, and if the majority are placing high value on reaching people outside the church, then they will be happy to give towards that vision.

More than that, God is faithful. You may not agree totally with this next statement but I say the faithfulness of God is sometimes dependent on the faith of the leader. Your Aunt and I have often looked back over events in our lives and said to one another, 'who would have thought?' Who would have thought it possible that God would orchestrate circumstances that blessed us, use our background and journey to bless others, take us places we never thought possible, and bring people into our lives who have enriched us beyond measure. But if I can say it without pride, His faithfulness to us was in some measure facilitated by our willingness to exercise our faith in Him.

A biblical example for me is when the disciples saw Jesus walking on water. Peter was trusting enough to get out of the boat and walk towards the Lord. His faith did falter when he saw the waves, but God was faithful even in that situation. I bet that when they got back in the boat the other disciples said something like 'I wish I had done that' or 'next time I'm going to do that', but the fact is they missed an opportunity to experience God's faithfulness, and if I read Scripture right they never had another opportunity to experience it in that way. There is no other record of walking on water. I know that God's faithfulness is not dependent on our actions, but it sure seems as if we might miss out on things that He has for us because we are unwilling to trust Him fully.

Enough from me, you have a family and a congregation to care for. And a soul of your own to feed. God Bless You.

Eldon

Daniel Donford

From: danield@charis.net
Sent: Tuesday 24 June, 9:08 a.m.
To: eldon@charis.net
Subject: Surprise Visitor

Dear Uncle Eldon,

I'm still not sure how it happened, but I survived my first year in pastoral ministry. And how my perspective has changed! Looking back now I can't believe how naïve I was when I first began. Some of my notions were preposterous. The other day I came across the templates I filled in from Schneider's book. According to my forecasts, the church was supposed to have doubled in size by now! Today I'm just pleased that it's stayed about the same. I suppose my misconceptions and mistakes haven't been too damaging then, which is a miracle really. It's just possible we've all grown from them. I know I have, though it was very painful along the way. There were moments when I really thought I wasn't going to make it. After all, I practically resigned, didn't I? Things seemed so very dark, so bleak. I shudder to think of it now, when I can see I've got a lot to be grateful for. Hayley has stood by me through all my ups and downs. And you've always been there to say exactly the right thing at precisely the right time. I don't know what I'd do without you.

Every now and then I go back through everything you've written (I've kept all your messages) and find myself encouraged all over again. Every thought you share has been seasoned by so much experience and I've tried to put it all into practice as best I can. One thing I've been working on lately is boundaries. I saw the sense in what you were saying and I think Hayley and I have created some good boundaries for our next year in ministry. To start with, we're going on vacation for three glorious weeks – the first break in twelve months. Boy, do we need it. We're driving over to the coast to stay at Silent Sound where we'll do nothing but reading and fishing and playing with the kids. Can't wait. Then when we get back we're moving out of the parsonage. It's too close to the church, so that when I'm away I'm not really away. Work whispers to me. So the church is going to rent a house for us three blocks over. I think the physical separation will be healthy. I'm looking forward to it. And we'll be getting our weekends back. Well, sort of. We negotiated with the Elders to have Fridays and Saturdays off. I think that will also give us some space. One-day breaks aren't enough to really wind down. Church is always looming just ahead, so two days in a row should provide much more balance. We'll even be able to go away for long weekends now and then, which will be good as well.

So things are looking up, but I haven't told you the best bit yet. Last night there was a knock on the door, late in the evening. Who should it be but Carmel Schumacher, Frank's widow. She came to tell us that she was moving away to live with her oldest daughter in Carrington. I must admit I shuddered to hear it, since she'll be taking Frank's money with her. But I needn't have worried. She handed me an envelope with a cheque for $120,000. She said that she liked what was happening in the church – the new ideas, the energy. And then she said that I remind her of Frank when he was my age. (Well that was a dismal thought and I renewed my resolve not to go the way of the Franks of this world.) And then she said that Frank thought I was the man to lead the church forward. I don't know what shocked me more, the cheque in my hand or the words in my ears. Yet in an odd way, I suppose it's possible. I guess one thing I've learned this year is that our judgments of people are nearly always wrong. We're either too generous or too critical. Carmel and Hayley were both crying by this point, and I was all stirred up myself. When I gave Carmel a hug it felt like I was making my peace with Frank as well.

So Carmel has moved away, but we're staying. Her gift will help to make the renovations to the church building. And with the new space and shape of our lives, I think Hayley and I are in for a good year ahead.

I hope you and Aunt Ethel are getting a break yourselves. And thanks again for all your wisdom and support over the last twelve months. God surely knew how much I needed it.

Dan

Uncle Eldon

From: eldon@charis.net
Sent: Friday 27 June, 2:28 p.m.
To: danield@charis.net
Subject: Re: Surprise Visitor

Dan:

Congratulations on your first year in pastoral ministry. You describe it as 'surviving' but I think it has been much more than that. While the dreams and expectations that you had twelve months ago may not have been fulfilled, the fact is that God has been honoured by your obedience to Him and your commitment to follow Him despite the circumstances. He has used you to bring fruit that will last for eternity and has brought honour to His name. And you have grown so much yourself. Well done.

Your latest email is almost like an annual review and I commend that practice to you in the years ahead. As I read it, it speaks to me of growth in your life through acknowledgment of mistakes you have made, of staying the course, and of a hunger to learn. These three things are attributes that I pray you never lose.

You also report good insights into the value of building relationships with the people you serve. The church is blessed to have you as a shepherd.

This is the time for you to put a candle on a cake and celebrate a milestone in ministry. Happy Birthday!

Eldon

Conflicts

Daniel Donford

From:	danield@charis.net
Sent:	Sunday 13 July, 9:08 p.m.
To:	eldon@charis.net
Subject:	A Letter

Oh, Uncle Eldon!

We had such a good vacation, but within an hour of getting home I feel like I need another one. The stunning peace of Silent Sound was shattered by a letter we found waiting for us when we got back. It's unsigned, anonymous, and only a page, but boy does it stab to the heart. I felt ill when I read it. I'm still getting over the shock, and I need you to tell me what to do with it. I guess I don't need to copy it out for you – I'll just hit the highlights.

Their big issue is with me. More particularly, whoever wrote it says I've got an 'anger problem'. And it's not just them: 'a lot of people in the church' believe the same thing. There's been steady talk about it behind my back, they say. People are unhappy with the way I've been leading the church. They say my style reflects deep personal issues and that I'm just pushing my own agenda. So it goes back to the way I tried to move the church forward in those early months, and especially to my outburst against Doris Blackmore. They come back to that several times in the letter. They think my anger is the product of unconfessed sin in my life, which is blocking my relationship with God. At the end of it all there's a list of fifteen Bible verses that I presume are on the subject of anger. They suggest that I make them the focus of study and prayer.

Well, I'm praying all right! That's the first thing I did. I was driven to my knees by a weight of terror I have never known. I had visions of me having to offer up my resignation, just at the moment when I felt most like staying! It might still come to that, if so many people are against me.

I've been trying to figure out who might have written it. Perhaps it was the Comptons, since they've hardly been on my side. Then Clive Philpott looked at me funny the last Sunday before our vacation. I didn't pay too much attention to it at the time, but now I wonder. And what if the talk got as far as Carlton and Stafford? I've been building up a good relationship with them over the last few months, but I can see how this might set it back. What if they think there's something in it? It isn't possible that one of them wrote it, is it? They're Elders, after all. So who did write it? Really, I have no idea! I can't believe how not knowing makes it all so much worse. It could be anyone. How can I look people in the eye without wondering if they're the ones who wrote this note? How will I be able to trust anyone, and how will I find out what's been going on? The whole thing has had weeks to fester, with us being away on vacation. I can't think how many others have been drawn into it by now. What few supporters I have might have turned against me, and who can blame them? I haven't always carried myself with the grace and patience of Christ, have I? My response to Doris Blackmore still haunts me, even more now. Perhaps I do have an anger problem.

So what do I do? Where do I start? I've gotten myself in such a mess. How do I get myself out?

I guess I have to face the office tomorrow. I feel sick to my stomach just thinking about it. You know, as Hayley and I were driving home with the kids we were genuinely excited about what lay ahead. We shared all these ideas for what we could do. I even began to wonder if I might make it in this church after all, that it could become a close community in which we feel loved and supported. Now I don't feel any of that. It's all been eaten away by the acid reality awaiting us at home. I suppose I'll wrestle with this all night, then face the office in the morning. Perhaps there's something I can rescue out of all the rubble.

More than ever, I'll be grateful for any advice you can offer. Have you ever dug yourself in this deep?

I hope you sleep better than I will.

Dan

Uncle Eldon

From: eldon@charis.net
Sent: Monday 14 July, 10:06 a.m.
To: danield@charis.net
Subject: Re: A Letter

Dan:

I'm glad you had a good vacation and that Silent Sound is still a place of 'stunning peace'. I hope you were able to tuck a few good books into your mind and enjoy the time with the family.

Knowing how refreshing a good vacation can be makes me even more disappointed that your return home was marked by such a vicious anonymous letter, a stab to the heart as you put it.

I find it helpful to start the processing of these things with a quick review of what I know to be true, as opposed to what some unknown person wants me to believe is true. In your case that is pretty clear. You inherited a somewhat dysfunctional church; you confronted some unhealthy people and situations; you made some mistakes, owned them and rectified them; you saw people change from an inward focus to a focus that faces the community and the world they live in; you had people embrace your vision; your Elders have grown with you; and a year later you are in a good position, poised to move ahead in ways that will honour the Lord.

Now comes this letter. People who are walking closely with the Lord and who feel your leadership is inadequate will handle their concerns God's way. That, according to Scripture, involves coming to see you and outlining their concerns over issues while affirming you as a brother in Christ, and a leader in the church who is worthy of, in your case, double honour. When it happens like this you know their name, you can look them in the eye, and see their concern for the church of God. Sometimes they may lack the courage to come personally so they write a letter that speaks the truth in love and they sign their name to it, and invite your response.

People who would be described in Scripture as 'carnal' write unsigned letters. I would call them carnal cowards, who think they can control others by threats and accusations. I've come across them in my time and found them to be very predictable. They accuse you of lacking some area of self-control, they claim to be just one of many who have the same opinion, they identify you as a control freak, and they spiritualize the whole thing and claim they have an inside track to God's mind. The one thing they are smart at is knowing that their letter will play tricks with your mind and they will find pleasure in watching your discomfort as you process what they wrote.

You have to choose. You can spend your days analyzing every word they wrote to see if you really are as they say, and then spend your nights trying to work out who it is who wrote it. Or you can choose to commit your way unto the Lord, trust in Him with all your heart and watch Him direct your paths. Lean on Him rather than on your own understanding. Do the latter and I predict you will see few people leave the church and many new people come, you will have a peace from God that will inspire you to lead the people with confidence and integrity, and before too long the writer of the letter will be revealed through some act of anger, the result of seeing the leader they wanted to destroy instead growing as a man of God and enjoying much fruit in ministry.

Taking the letter and actually burning it is helpful. A brave man might also report the matter to the church publicly, asking for prayer for someone who would do such a thing. I was never that brave.

Don't let anyone steal the benefits of your time at Silent Sound. Approach the Lord of the church with humility and ask Him to give you renewed confidence as you start this new year of ministry. You are in the right place in your right mind. Don't get angry, that would validate the writer of the letter.

Lead on.

Eldon

Daniel Donford

From:	danield@charis.net
Sent:	Thursday 31 July, 10:07 a.m.
To:	eldon@charis.net
Subject:	Encouragement

Dear Uncle Eldon,

I can't tell you how helpful your last email was. I read it in wonder. By the end of it I felt an amazing liberation. I think the anonymous letter had become instantly oppressive and terrifying to me. Thinking on it now, I can see that it really did mess with my mind. I almost can't believe how badly it unhinged me, but I'm very pleased to say that I write this email in a much better place.

It's been an encouraging couple of weeks. Soon after I received the letter I had coffee with Sam Campbell. I've really enjoyed building our relationship, and we've started to go a little bit deeper in our conversations with each other. It's great to have someone around who's been in pastoral ministry longer than I have (which I know is just about everyone in pastoral ministry). He actually laughed out loud when I told him about the anonymous note and, like you, he suggested that I burn it. I did. I went straight home and burnt the thing. Hayley and I watched it crumble away into ash. (That felt really good!) I didn't go so far as to tell the church about it, mainly because Carlton and Stafford were so supportive, and because we found out who wrote it: the Murkowskis.

I don't think I've mentioned them to you before. Tony and Eleanor Murkowski are an older couple who left the church a while back, I think, but who have come more regularly over the last few months. He has this beak nose and narrow eyes, and I can hardly say that I warmed to him. There was just something about him that made me uneasy, but I can't put my finger on it. He looked at me with a touch of contempt, but that may have been the shape of his face. He hardly looks like Santa Claus. His wife Eleanor is very refined and quite tall, much taller than he is, and intimidating with it. I tended to give them a wide berth, I have to say. Stafford Krinks did some investigating and quickly worked out they were behind the letter. Thankfully, he and Carlton were the ones to confront them. They admitted to sending it, and Stafford thought he was able to talk them round. So we can put that episode behind us (though I admit I avoid looking at them when I preach).

And then I had this dazzling conversation with Clive Philpott. I now shake my head to think I had him on my list of possible letter writers. In fact, he's really coming on board with things. I have Carmel Schumacher to thank for that. When Clive heard about her gift he could see that change might just be possible around here. He's also getting the point. He told me that in the past he's thought several times of inviting his new neighbour (I think he's called Larry) over to church, but has never actually done it because he's worried Larry would find it all too foreign and – this was Clive's word – 'weird'. Clive hopes we can make it all more accessible. He even thinks he might enjoy that himself – 'Time we had a fresh breeze blow through here!' I couldn't agree more. And it's not just Clive Philpott who is coming around to that point of view. I must admit, I'm inspired.

So I think I've learned a few more lessons out of it all. One of the biggest is that when something awful happens it's never as bad as it first appears. It is incredible to think how quickly my mind ran away with itself when I read that awful letter, imagining the very worst of all possibilities. But none of them came to pass. Perspective is a wonderful thing. It would be nice to think I could approach the next crisis with this balanced perspective from the start, but perhaps that's asking too much. What I need to remember is that this is God's church. He says to the waves, 'This far and no further'. While I might get turned upside down in the breakers, God has set his limits.

Can you believe it? Here I am offering you some of *my* wisdom!! I'm sure it's something you learned a very long time ago, but it's helpful for me to write it down, and it's encouraging to think I've grown a little. It's so good to have you to talk to about these things.

Dan

Martha Krinks

From: martha_krinks@endora.com
Sent: Monday 25 August, 7:42 p.m.
To: jdandemtrout@vmail.org
Subject: Re: Recipe

My dear Janice,

I think I have attached the recipe that you asked for and I am really so sorry that it took me so long to send it through. I had to wait for Stafford to show me how, and he doesn't have too many spare moments. He is so excited about all that is happening in the church these days he looks like a new man, he really does. You know he used to drag himself out the door to Elders' meetings and now he hurries away to them. I was lucky to get his help tonight before he went to another one, otherwise you might never have seen the recipe. I do hope your dinner party goes well. I have found that it pays to let the chowder simmer for a long while to really bring out the taste.

Give my love to Ed.

Martha

Daniel Donford

From:	danield@charis.net
Sent:	Tuesday 23 September, 3:03 p.m.
To:	eldon@charis.net
Subject:	Hiking

Dear Uncle Eldon,

It feels like ages since I last wrote to you. As always, the weeks have had their ups and downs, though sometimes it feels like there are more downs than ups. About a month ago the gossip about my 'anger problem' resurfaced, just when I thought it had been left in the past. Do you remember Alice, the young lady from the youth group? She had let it slip to Hayley that plenty of people are murmuring behind our backs. She said that her cousin had been talking to her friend who had heard her mother tell some unknown friend on the phone all about my character issues. And she's not the only one. I took some dry cleaning into a shop last week and the lady who served me – she comes to church now and then – gave me this very strange look. What was she thinking, I wonder?

So there I was, down in the dumps again. Looking back on it now, the feelings were different somehow. I had this sense that things were unraveling all around me. I'm not sure I have ever felt more estranged from the church than I did just then. I felt distanced from the people, detached, and unwelcome in my own church. I didn't know who was against me and who was for me; who had been talking about me and who might have dared to speak up in my defense. I must admit that was another real low point for me.

I was on the verge of sending you a message when I had to leave for an Elders' meeting. They have been so encouraging lately. Carlton and Stafford have really come to life. There is a light in their eyes that I am sure wasn't there before. I think they're enjoying the experience of seeing God at work in the church. After years in which the movements of his Spirit seemed so sporadic and small they are invigorated by the new breeze that is blowing through the place. I think almost everybody is, but it means something different to Carlton and Stafford who have been in a leadership position for a while now. They are growing – really growing. Again, I think we all are, and it's so rewarding, so satisfying to be a part of it.

At that meeting we decided to go hiking, just the three of us. This summer has been a good one and the weather held for a couple more weeks. We drove into the back of the Coverdale Hills then climbed through the Pinnacles onto Stoneyback Ridge. There is a cabin there that overlooks Lake Langton and the Greendale Valley. We stayed up long into the night just talking and encouraging each other. The light of the fire seemed to draw us out. Somehow I found the courage to broach the issue of my own anger with them. I asked them to tell me honestly if they thought I had a problem with it. They were both so affirming and encouraging, but they were honest with it. The good news is that they don't think I have an anger problem – they could see the pressure I was under when I yelled at Doris Blackmore. But they lightly put their finger on one or two other issues that I do need to address. I guess it hurt a little to hear it, but I also felt loved and respected and built up all at the same time. After we talked about me for a while, Carlton asked us to touch on any issues in his life that need addressing. Then Stafford asked for our assessment of him. I can't recall a single moment in my life when I felt so close to other guys. It will stay in my mind as a very precious memory. After we had talked for a long while we prayed for each other. I read from the prayer of Jesus in John 17:22 where he asked 'that they may be one as we are one'. Right at that moment I felt like his prayer had been answered.

We should go hiking more often.

Dan

Daniel Donford

From:	danield@charis.net
Sent:	Saturday 25 October, 10:07 p.m.
To:	eldon@charis.net
Subject:	Renovations

Dear Uncle Eldon,

There's something inspiring about tangible change. Over the last few weeks we've been making some renovations to the church, which is so exciting. We're underway at last! Do you know, one evening before it all began Hayley and I came into the church with a sledgehammer. Really! I'd asked the builders if we could, and they said go ahead. So Hayley and I took it in turns to bang holes in the plaster. We didn't do much – pretty soon we collapsed next to each other in laughter and tears – but boy, did it feel good! What a precious moment. We wiped away the tears and asked God for grace, that he might bring new life and light into the church through the changes we were planning.

I think he's answering our prayer, I really do! The renovations have really pulled us together as a church. Everyone was involved, from the youth group through to Harold and Meredith – who I have to say have really become quite a couple. They were there the whole way through, working as a team at whatever needed doing. In church they always sit together, quietly commenting and sniggering like school children. (I think Harry Compton is relieved that he can now sit through a church service without constant interruptions from his elderly aunt.) A few weeks ago we all had a barn dance out at a farm on the outskirts of town, owned by another old guy called Ted Saunders. It was a great evening, not just for how many people in the church were there, but for how many of them had brought along their friends and neighbours. The place was packed. At one point they needed two people to demonstrate some new dance steps, and who should volunteer but Meredith and Harold. They were such a comical sight but really quite lovely, dancing around with the energy of teenagers. It was fun just watching them and I'm sure the caller kept the demonstration going longer than he needed to.

But I digress. Thanks to some astute work by the deacons, we've made Carmel's money go a very long way. Not only that, we had a special offering that brought in another $38,000. I had no idea there was so much money in the church, and so much willingness to provide for what God is doing. So we've been able to extend the church by about twenty feet, which means we can realign the seating so that we're facing sideways to the way we were before. We've bought some individual chairs to replace the pews and we've installed a bank of windows on the south side that let in a lot more light. The place seems airy and spacious and new, especially now we've painted it. That's what we've been doing these last few weeks. People have spent hours down there, helping out, painting, cleaning. It's amazing, and such a tonic for me. I don't feel at all disconnected now. I guess I overestimated the grumblers, and as far as I can tell the gossip about me has stopped. Of course, the Murkowskis didn't show up once, which probably made the difference, and they don't look very happy about the changes. Well, I'm not worried. I suppose I could confront them about the gossip, but I'm too much of a coward and it seems to have blown over. Truth to tell, I'm quietly hoping they'll leave. Is that bad?

Oh, I didn't tell you the best bit. Do you remember me mentioning Clive Philpott's neighbour, Larry? He's the one Clive thought about inviting to church. Well, it turns out he's a builder, and he's given us a lot of his time as well. He's spent hours and hours working with us down at the church. He looks more comfortable there every day. He's even talked about coming to the opening service. We hadn't thought of having one! But if he wants to come, we'll lay it on.

I really think God is on the move, and not just in the building project. Doris and Andrew Blackmore have agreed they want to work on their marriage, and not give up. They look more relaxed with each other than I've seen them in ages. I know there's still an awful lot for them to work through yet, but I think there may be hope. It's amazing how important relationships have become to me. I'm overjoyed to see this one might be on the mend. (At the very least, it's great to preach without Doris's eyes boring into me!)

So there's plenty to encourage. I shared it all with Sam Campbell, my pastor friend, and he was very affirming. It's always good to learn from him, but this time there was a new respect in his eyes. I must admit, that felt good. Now that I think about it, he said he had something important to share, but he never mentioned it in the end. Maybe I talked too much! Oh well, next time.

Look at the clock! I might have a long soak in the tub, wash off the last flecks of paint, then go to bed. Thanks again for joining me in this great work. You and Aunt

Ethel should come and visit sometime, see what we're doing with the place.

Dan

Uncle Eldon

From:	eldon@charis.net
Sent:	Tuesday 28 October, 3:34 p.m.
To:	danield@charis.net
Subject:	Re: Renovations

Dan:

Thank you for the latest update. It really is a privilege to have a young Pastor willing to share his heart as you do. And all I am doing in return is sharing from life experiences along a path that may have similarities to your own. God has been good and taught me many things, often painful but always for my good.

Now, the Murkowskis. Apparently they are still gossiping and you hope they will leave. Is that bad you ask? The answer is yes.

Leading a church can be likened to driving a train. People at various times will join your train and leave your train. Some stay on board for a lifetime, most get off after a few years. Leaving is prompted by changed life circumstances, new desires, dissatisfaction. Hopefully it is God who leads them off your train; it is not just their human desires or reactions prompting them to disembark. As a leader your role is not to lock the doors and keep them on your train, your role is to take them on a journey that leads them closer to the destination God has for them (to be more like Him). The worst thing you can do is have them join a stationary train. You must move them forward while they are under your care.

The Murkowskis need to be confronted about behaviour that keeps them from being all that God wants for them. Right now they are on your train and so the responsibility for alerting them to that fact falls to you. To let them leave your train without them facing that road block (or train block) is tantamount to having them sitting on a train for several years without going anywhere. Good leaders won't let that happen.

Confrontation is hard. Make sure you confront the issue, don't attack the person. You are on solid biblical ground as you point out the destructive nature of gossip for them and for the wider body of Christ. If you do this, you will be helping them and you will be helping the church even if they choose to leave after your confrontation. Choose not to deal with it and you will not only have done a disservice to the Murkowskis, but you will have allowed a seed to sprout in the culture of your church that will produce more sub-standard behaviour.

One more thing: because confrontation is tough, you want to deal with it just once. Don't hold back and make subtle suggestions, talk to them directly and fully, calling for acknowledgment of their sin and repentance from it. Set in place some ways of measuring their response, and set standards for them to attain in their life in the church. Like surgery, you want to be sure you have identified and removed all of the dangerous material. You don't want a recurrence – deal with it fully the first time.

Sorry to sound like a stern old man, but I write in love. And with memories of regret that I didn't always confront in my ministry according to the words I have just written you.

Go to it. You are loved, affirmed and prayed for.

Eldon

Daniel Donford

From:	danield@charis.net
Sent:	Wednesday 19 November, 9:38 a.m.
To:	eldon@charis.net
Subject:	Gossip

Dear Uncle Eldon,

Sometimes it seems a different church from one week to the next! When I wrote to you last we seemed so together as we worked on the renovations. The Murkowskis were just an uncomfortable, bitter, nagging presence in the back of my mind. I hoped I could ignore it. No way, and not for long. That root of gossip you mentioned has spread its tendrils underground, and only now that it's come to the surface can I see just how far it's spread. Over the last few days three of my fellow saints have trooped round to tell me that 'a lot of people' in the church were talking about my 'anger problem'. Why, oh why, did I ever allow myself that outburst at Doris Blackmore last year? And when will it stop coming back round to bite me? Apparently, people are afraid to come and see me with their concerns for fear they might get the same response, as if I'm this slightly insane pastor always on the edge of an angry tirade!

I can trace all of it back to the Murkowskis, and I plan to take your advice. I loved your image of pastor as train driver. I can see my responsibility in that. I can't let the Murkowskis sit in a side track even if the thought of confronting them fills me with a sharp dread. So I will gather all the courage I possess and arrange a meeting with them.

If there's any encouragement for me in all that's happening, it's that I think I'm growing. I must admit that the last eighteen months or so have been a bewildering experience. It's just not what I thought. You know, I never had enemies until I became a pastor. I'd never seen what a church – a church! – can do to someone. Sometimes it has left me completely shattered. I've felt like my identity and expectations and assumptions are lying like precious, fragile shards on the ground, in danger of being trampled into fine dust and with no chance of reassembly. Yet I do feel I am being reassembled, and I like what's taking shape. I look back on myself even a year ago and think I would have responded differently to my current predicament. I can remember being so offended by one of your early emails – now I'm grateful when you tell me exactly what I need to know. I keep a lookout for what God is doing in the midst of the chaos. And I try to remember my own advice – as bad as it seems, it's probably not as bad as it seems. But I don't know what I'd do if I didn't have you to keep me steady. And the more I read the books you sent, the more I grow. I still keep Sidney Schneider on the shelf, but that's where he stays these days. I hear he's coming through to Sandarosa Falls next month, but I don't think I'll go. There's too much to do round here.

I'd better finish up. I'm supposed to be resting my ankle after I sprained it yesterday. It's still pretty swollen and bruised. I tripped over Meredith while she was lying on the floor. She does that a lot and I suppose I should expect it by now, but she always appears just when I least expect her. I very nearly uttered some words a pastor should not speak.

Back to the bed rest, then.

Dan

Daniel Donford

From:	danield@charis.net
Sent:	Wednesday 19 November, 7:43 p.m.
To:	eldon@charis.net
Subject:	Re: Re: Gossip

Dear Uncle Eldon,

I can understand your confusion. What I have clearly failed to mention is that Meredith is our new cat. I finally conceded defeat, worn down by the implacable determination of my family. Three weeks ago we traipsed off to the pet store and came back home an hour later a fair bit poorer and with our new kitten carried in Emily's arms. The first thing we discussed was a name for it, and I suggested we call it Meredith. I really was only joking – my effort at black humour – but Emily took my suggestion in both hands and would not let it go. Nothing that Hayley or I could say would make her budge. She really is very strong-willed, that girl. Sometimes I wonder what kind of teenager we will have on our hands in just a few years.

We were a bit worried about what Meredith Bellweather would think of having a cat named after her. We shouldn't have been concerned. She was honoured and delighted, and she fussed over that kitten as if we'd just brought a third child home from the hospital. Meredith (the human) is really quite lovely once you get to know her. She is eccentric, that's for sure, and I cannot fathom her thing with cats. But she's also a very godly woman, if unconventional. I know that she spends hours every day on her knees praying fervently, often for me. The Lord knows how much I need it.

As for Meredith the cat, well, I don't find her nearly so charming. It's as though she has worked out that of all the people in the house I like her the least, so she fixes me with the most attention. She is constantly wanting to jump on my lap, or sticking her claws in my ankles to get my attention. I can't tell you how many times I have been deep in concentration only to be wrenched back to reality by a vicious stinging in my extremities. And yesterday was the limit, it really was. If I hadn't been sprawled on the floor in agony, incapacitated and immobile, that might just have been the end of her.

Dan

Daniel Donford

From:	danield@charis.net
Sent:	Monday 15 December, 11:11 a.m.
To:	eldon@charis.net
Subject:	Questions

Dear Uncle Eldon,

Over the last few weeks I've been making a list of questions that I just don't get. Like this one: Why are things never perfect, even in a church? Why is it that the church seems just as broken and fallen as any other institution? Why is it that when I look at the local Rotary Club I don't see anything like the disunity and dysfunction you can see in a church regularly enough? What was God thinking? Is this really what he had in mind?

Questions. They're not hard to come up with. It's the answers that are difficult, and I don't know quite what to make of those. I guess I need to accept that while it remains in this world, the church is, like any other institution or body, fallen. I recall someone saying that we are all like paintings: we look good from a distance, but the closer we get, the more flaws we see. And it's the pastor who gets closest of all to the flaws inside a church, since he lives so much on the inside. It seems a place of such vulnerability, where determination has to fight off disillusionment. It's also a place where wounds are inflicted, hidden, dark, and veiled from the rest of the community, but all the deeper for it.

Sorry, I'm getting morbid. Hayley is usually around to encourage me, but she's taken the children to visit her mother. I was going to have coffee with Sam Campbell but he rang up to cancel. So it's just you and me today. You're stuck with my questions. If you have any answers, I'd be fascinated to hear them. Actually, I can imagine you pointing me to him who endured the greatest, deepest wounds of all from the people he called his own. If it was enough for him to endure, it's enough for me. It's just that sometimes there seems little prospect of joy to propel me forward.

You might be wondering what has brought all this about. Fatigue, more than likely, but also recent events in which we plunged from the sublime to the ridiculous, like going from a sauna to an ice bath. I have to say our official opening was a grand success. Clive's neighbour, Larry, was there along with some of his family and even a few of his friends. There were also lots of other new faces. It was so invigorating and refreshing. Hayley and I had formed a small committee to shape the service, and we had so much fun putting it together. It went off beautifully. There was such an atmosphere! I was all ready to frame it in my mind and hold the memory forever.

Then the crash. Just as I was locking up, Carlton and Stafford came over to see me. They said there were still grumbles about my 'anger problem' and that someone – they didn't say who – had asked for a meeting to talk about it. I can't tell you how disappointed I felt. Coming after the high point of the opening service I was crestfallen and crushed.

Carlton and Stafford must have sensed how low I was. They suggested that they organize a meeting and run it themselves, without me present. They thought people might speak more freely if I wasn't there. I felt a stab in my heart about that, like it was a rejection. A little voice warned me I should face up to this myself. I remembered your advice about confronting those who need confronting. But I just didn't have it in me to argue the point with Carlton and Stafford, and I felt grateful and relieved by their offer. At least I knew that they understood me and supported me. I let it go.

Perhaps I shouldn't have done that, but it worked out okay in the end. They had the meeting last night. From what I hear, Carlton stood his ground magnificently. (He and Stafford have grown so much this year, it's amazing.) And Harold told the people a few home truths! I was so encouraged to hear that. And get this, Harold told Carlton why the Murkowskis are out to get me. Years ago, Tony Murkowski applied for the position of pastor and Frank turned him down. He's nursed a grudge ever since. So with Frank off the scene, Tony turned up gunning for the job. That's why he wants me out – so he can be pastor. I have to admit, knowing his agenda makes the whole thing more manageable. Having Harold as an ally is a great boost. And the meeting ended on a positive note.

So I think we can say that episode is now over and we can all move on.

What are you and Aunt Ethel doing for Christmas? We're having Alice (from the youth group) and her mother around for Christmas dinner. I'm looking forward to it. Alice is really growing in her faith.

Dan

Daniel Donford

From:	danield@charis.net
Sent:	Monday 15 December, 12:33 p.m.
To:	eldon@charis.net
Subject:	Another Question

Dear Uncle Eldon,

I've just been pottering around the house doing a bit of tidying up. (I wonder if it's best to tidy as I go or do one big clean-up at the end. I still haven't quite decided but I think I'll take a cautious approach. I'd like to show Hayley how accomplished I can be on the domestic front and it won't help things to come back to a big mess if my carefully laid plans to restore cleanliness at the last minute get disrupted. Mind you, if I look too proficient I might find myself on the end of a vacuum cleaner more often.)

Anyway, while I've been doing all this I've been thinking some more. I can now see that there's far more discouragement involved in this pastoring business than I ever realized. When I think back on the last few weeks, somehow it's the dark and depressing moments that linger in my mind and seem to have most effect. I still get that sick feeling whenever I think back to what Carlton and Stafford told me about the ongoing gossip. It's hardly going to be the last discouraging moment I'll ever have in my life, is it?

So here's my question: how should I cope with discouragement? Simple question really. It's the answer that's the challenge.

Time for some lunch…

Dan

Uncle Eldon

From:	eldon@charis.net
Sent:	Tuesday 16 December, 3:34 p.m.
To:	danield@charis.net
Subject:	Re: Another Question

Dan:

It may be a simple question, but I am glad you raised it because it is an issue that doesn't seem to go away even after years of ministry. And I have noticed a sense of discouragement in your words and tone recently. This is not uncommon in ministry as the initial wave of excitement, achievement and affirmation of others begins to fade. As they often say in ministry, 'the honeymoon is over'. I rather like that analogy because it indicates the agreement between the Pastor and the people can be healthier when it is seen more as a relationship like a marriage than simply an employment agreement.

Discouragement is like sand in the shoes. I remember reading the account of a man who walked across the USA from east coast to west. It took what seemed forever, wore out many pairs of shoes, and was a feat that attracted media attention at the end. The question was asked: 'Did you ever want to give up?' and the answer was 'almost daily'. So was it the loneliness of the Appalachians, the wind and dust of the prairies, the snow in the Rockies, the heat of Arizona? 'None of those', was his reply. 'It was the daily sand in my shoes.'

So it is with the church. The thing that takes most leaders out of ministry is not the massive public blowout, it is the daily sand of discouragement that makes the personal walk too hard to bear. Dealing with people as constantly and intimately as you do, will inevitably result in doubt about your self-worth and identity. We must learn how to separate our work for God from our walk with God, for it is our personal relationship with God that will sustain us when the work for God falls apart.

Years ago during a time of self-pity in ministry, a colleague of mine invited me to walk with him and share my discouraged heart. I remember it clearly: we stopped by a lake at one point, he put his hand on my shoulders and told me that God's desire was to humble me, refine me and deepen me. Only a few people at that time were close enough to say that and have me take it to heart, another reason to develop close and deep relationships. Focusing on God's desires for me rather than on my own ambitions has allowed me to complete my own spiritual journey from east to west without succumbing to the loneliness, wind, snow and heat of ministry. It has also helped me to see that the constant removal of discouraging sand from the shoes is a necessary part of leading others on their spiritual journey.

The beautiful words of Moses spoken to the people of Israel have probably been used by you to bless your congregation at the end of Sunday worship. I suggest you take a moment to shine them into your soul and find the encouragement you need:

> The Lord bless you and keep you.
> The Lord make His face to shine upon you and be gracious to you.
> The Lord turn His face toward you, and give you His peace.

A shining face will be a regular part of your pastoral journey as you watch the people you serve: in the bridegroom and the bride joining hands to make their vows; in the young couple bringing their newborn to you for prayer; in the parents introducing their adult child who has come home after some major accomplishment or service. Such shining faces bring encouragement and joy.

Similarly, the Lord's face shines on you as He sees you for who you are: a part of His bride, His precious and valuable child, and His faithful and fruitful worker accomplishing something that brings glory to Him. And so His face is turned towards you, He gives you His full attention, He is devoted to you, He gives you His peace.

Don't look away at a time like this. Thank Him and allow Him to humble you in His presence, refine you daily into His likeness, and deepen you in your understanding of His love for you. He desires to bless you and keep you.

May His grace and peace be yours in abundance,

Eldon

Harry Compton

From:	hjcompton@compton.com
Sent:	Wednesday 17 December, 9:21 p.m.
To:	murkowskis@griblet.org
Subject:	Re: Meeting

Tony,

Don't blame me for that meeting! That was all your fault. You shouldn't have come on so strong at the beginning, so don't lecture me about saying my bit. Can't you see that he has some strong support in the church? Who'd have thought he'd have done so well or lasted so long around here!

I thought you would provide some leadership for the church. Now I'm not sure you can.

So back off.

Harry

Sam Campbell

From:	samcampbell368@icarus.com
Sent:	Tuesday 27 January, 8:52 a.m.
To:	danield@charis.net
Subject:	Sick

Hey Dan.

I'm sick. I've come down with the flu or something. So I can't meet up for coffee today like we planned. I'm disappointed because there's something I really need to talk to you about. I'll send you an email when I'm better and we'll reschedule.

Sam

Daniel Donford

From:	danield@charis.net
Sent:	Sunday 1 February, 4:46 p.m.
To:	eldon@charis.net
Subject:	Amazing!

Dear Uncle Eldon,

There's some news I just have to share with you: Larry has come to faith! Clive Philpott burst into my office just half an hour ago to tell me. I don't think I've ever seen quite the same look on anyone else's face. He was so alive and animated and I'm not sure what to be more delighted about, Larry's first step on the journey or Clive's quantum leap. I can't help feeling that both of them are new men.

Here's the story: Larry has been reasonably successful in life. His building business, though still fairly small, has kept his family pretty well off over the years. But they've moved house a lot. Larry likes to renovate, so his wife, Rosie, has lived in a revolving shambles for twenty years or more. Finally she put her foot down. Refused to move any more. Likes the house they're in. Apparently she told Larry that if he wanted to shift again, he'd be doing it without her. I don't think she really meant it, but if she wanted to bring Larry to his senses, it worked. It seems he took a long hard look inside himself to see why he was always wanting to move on to the next house, the next project. He began to see that if the last one hadn't satisfied whatever urge was driving him, the next one was hardly going to do it either. Suddenly he faced a whole lot of big questions.

In the meantime, he'd been to church more freq
ly. Lately he's been coming every week. I've been preaching through Hebrews 11 for the last month or so. I started off by saying that, in the end, it is God that matters
most. Our relationship with God defines our life. Then
we moved into the stories of all those people who had
lived such purposeful lives of faith. I made sure we didn't
gloss over the price they paid, the suffering they experienced, the wounds they bore. I must say it was inspiring
enough for me, but it really had an impact on Larry. He
began yearning for that kind of courageous life. When
we finished the series this morning, we 'fixed our eyes
on Jesus' at the beginning of chapter 12. I think Larry's
eyes were opened. He practically dragged Clive out to
lunch to talk about it, which they did, for three hours. In
the course of the conversation, Larry's life was radically
realigned.

Clive stopped in on the way home to fill me in, and
he's changed too. I'm not sure if he's ever seen the Spirit
of God move so dramatically around him. He could hardly believe that his everyday conversations with Larry
over the fence would bear such remarkable fruit. He had
no idea the life of faith could be this exciting. He's spent
a lifetime in church and it had all become very predictable and routine. These latest changes have breathed
fresh life into his faith. There's no telling how far Clive
will go from here, but I have a hunch what we're seeing
now is only the very beginning.

You know, when I look at Clive, and the changes in
him, it helps me to see the changes in me. I came here
with so many ludicrous expectations, I can see that now.
I envisaged growth simply in numerical terms. I had

exaggerated visions of turning this small community into a church of thousands. I entirely failed to conceive of growth in biological terms. Sure, the church is still much the same size as when I arrived, but how it has grown! We all have, through good times and bad. Now I don't mind if the church does blossom into the thousands, but I honestly don't mind if it doesn't. I just want to be faithful to what God has in mind. I've given up imagining my own preferred future. I just want to get in on what God is already doing. If the angels can rejoice when just one sinner is saved, so can I. I've been struck lately by the many small and everyday things Jesus used to describe the Kingdom of God: mustard seeds, wheat and soil. I think I can see now how God's work is accomplished in deceptively small measures. And that's enough for me.

It tops off a good week. On Monday evening I paid another visit to the youth group. They were so welcoming and appreciative. I was very humbled, especially when I saw Alice's shining face among them. I put aside the woeful memories of my first visit at that point. I'm just glad to be where I am now, not where I was then. This morning Harold Carmichael asked David if he was going to grow up to be a preacher, just like his dad. I must admit, the question didn't make me shudder like it used to. I don't mind what he grows up to do, but if he wants to be a pastor, I will think it a worthy calling.

And on Friday evening Hayley and I went out for dinner and a movie. We've been doing this a bit lately, to bring some balance into our ministry life and to invest in our relationship. Meredith Bellweather offered to babysit for us whenever we want, which is just great. Often Harold comes around to join her. They are both night owls and we never need to hurry home. So we saw this movie based on a true story about a guy who wanders into a cave that collapses behind him. He spent days digging his way back out. If that's a picture of my life, I think I might be on the verge of breaking back out into blue skies and fresh air. Though I guess that crisis is never far away in the life of a pastor.

Dan

Sam Campbell

From:	samcampbell368@icarus.com
Sent:	Tuesday 3 February, 2:37 p.m.
To:	danield@charis.net
Subject:	Trouble

Hey Dan.

Something's happened. It's bad. I'm in trouble – big trouble. I can't seem to get hold of you. Can you call me at home asap?

Sam

Martha Krinks

From: martha_krinks@endora.com
Sent: Tuesday 3 February, 8:52 p.m.
To: jdandemtrout@vmail.org
Subject: Teapots

My dear Janice,

Well I am fair worn out. I have spent most of the day taking down each and every one of my teapot collection and giving them all a good dust and clean. They really were so dirty I felt mortified I had let them get in such a state. Of course it wouldn't have taken me so long if not for the regular phone calls from others (there are so many who need nothing more than a good listening ear) and visitors calling around for coffee (I baked two cakes) and of course, there are so very many teapots that I have collected after all these years. Do you remember the one I bought in that old antique shop in North Bolton on that trip we took through the hill country there? That was such a good time wasn't it?

I was taking the chance to clean the teapots while Stafford is out of town. I really do think he does not even see the collection and he leaves it to me to look after. He has gone away for a few days with dear Daniel to some sort of pastoral care workshop or some such thing. Stafford did explain it to me but I can't quite remember the details. He thinks it will help him to become a better Elder and I have to say that ambition (don't the Scriptures call that a noble ambition?) is still growing in him. I really am so pleased that he has found such an encouraging companion in Daniel. I know they will be having a wonderful time together.

I don't think I told you that I will be seeing the grandchildren next week. I just can't wait. They are dears.

Do give my love to Ed.

Martha

Daniel Donford

From:	danield@charis.net
Sent:	Wednesday 4 February, 8:49 a.m.
To:	eldon@charis.net
Subject:	Workshop

Dear Uncle Eldon,

I thought I might send you a very quick note to say how much Hayley and I are enjoying your old friend Malcolm. He has such good stuff to say! Rest assured I haven't forgotten what you said about there being no easy or simple answers, so I haven't been looking for any. I used to think it could be that way – just find a formula that works and run with it – but if there's anything I've learned so far it's that pastoral ministry is richer and more complex and more demanding than I ever realized. It can't be franchised. Still, there is a lot to learn and it's helpful. And Malcolm knows a lot of it already so I'm paying careful attention. Some of his stories have included you, from when he worked as your assistant pastor. He claims that you taught him everything he needed to know. Of course he's gone on to a lot of other places since then, especially now he's chosen to invest most of his time in training young pastors, but I was very proud to introduce myself as your nephew.

Oh, the other thing is that Stafford is really enjoying it as well. It's been great to have him here with us to hear it all firsthand rather than me having to repeat it, which is never as effective. Sometimes I think he is more excited and inspired by these few days than I am, and that's saying something.

Anyway, I'd better dash. The next session starts in ten minutes, and I've just read an email from Sam Campbell asking me to ring him urgently. I should have time to do that now. I wonder what's up.

Dan

Sam Campbell

From: samcampbell368@icarus.com
Sent: Wednesday 4 February, 3:00 p.m.
To: danield@charis.net
Subject: Confession

Hey Dan.

Thanks for leaving the phone message. I'd forgotten that you were spending these few days with Malcolm. I guess I'll have to rely on email. In a way that's easier for me because what I have to say is very difficult. I need to warn you that what you're about to read is going to come as a shock. I hope you're sitting down.

I don't know where to start.

When I asked if we could get together regularly it was because I had a problem in my life that was starting to get out of control. At least, I couldn't control it no matter how much I tried. I hoped that by forming a friendship with you I might be able to open up to someone who could help, just by making me accountable. I was so stupid. I should have come out with it at the start but each time I tried to say the words I got scared and embarrassed. I told myself that we needed time to get to know each other before I landed you with this, that I was afraid you wouldn't understand. I think they may have been just excuses, I don't know. By the time we were due to meet up last week I was determined to come clean, but then I got sick and it all came out into the open.

I've been having some issues with my work computer. We have a guy in the church who looks after all our IT and I'd mentioned these problems to him. When I got sick he thought that would be a good chance to take the computer away to give it a good check-up while I wasn't needing it. As he was doing that he discovered what I'd been looking at on the internet.

Dan, I have developed an addiction to internet pornography. That was pretty clear from the evidence this guy assembled. He didn't know what to do about it. But he didn't come to me with it. Instead he told Mervin. I can't think of a worse choice. Mervin went straight to the other Elders. This Sunday they will announce to the church that I have been fired.

It's horrific. I can't tell you how bad it is. I feel sick to my stomach all the time. I can't sleep nights for thinking about it. Barbara has moved out with the kids. She feels hurt and humiliated. She's staying with her mother in Garrinsville. I don't know what she's thinking or if it's permanent. She says she just can't talk to me at the moment and I can understand that. So I'm in the house by myself, unemployed, with no one to talk to, and I'm wondering what on earth I'm going to do. And she's not the only one I've hurt. My congregation are going to feel betrayed. I'm the one who's supposed to set an example and I haven't done that. I keep having these thoughts of what they'll say and think and to be honest it all makes me cry, often. I haven't shed this many tears in years. I feel like I've lost everything. I don't know what's going to happen to me.

I've been such a fool. I can't believe the risks I took. My sin has certainly found me out, and it has ruined my life. It has surely ended my ministry.
I'd love to hear from you. I'm not sure anyone else wants to have anything to do with me right now.

Sam

Sam Campbell

From: samcampbell368@icarus.com
Sent: Wednesday 4 February, 10:13 p.m.
To: danield@charis.net
Subject: Thanks

Hey Dan.

It was really good to talk to you briefly. I want you to know how much it means to me that you are pre-pared to walk with me through this, and that you're coming home early. Please let me know the minute you arrive.

There is a little bit of good news. Barbara gave me a call this evening. She didn't say much. She thinks that it's not going to work for long staying at her mother's so she wants to come home and get the girls back into school. But she doesn't want me in the house with them, at least not yet. I can't tell you how painful the conversation was. I could hear the hurt and betrayal in every word she spoke. I tried to tell her that what happened wasn't a reflection on her or our relationship. I love Barbara. We have a great relationship. But it would have sounded hol-low to her.

So why did I do it? That's the question. You know, even I'm not sure I know the answer. But I'll try to explain it to you. It might help to sort out my own thinking, and perhaps you can learn something from my foolishness.

Like you, Dan, I find being a pastor very difficult at a personal level. I probably don't show it much, but it's true. There are no simple relationships. Everyone has their demands and expectations. Everyone wants a piece of me and I never worked out how to handle it.

My sin (and I know I have to call it that) started imperceptibly with a quick glance at fairly innocuous images, and it grew from there. I built my own world where I could have relationships that didn't make any demands on me, ones without complications, without criticism, without the usual give and take of a real relationship. I made choices and took small steps that led me little by little away from where I should have been. Once I cultivated the desire it was impossible to make it go away. Part of me loathed my sin, but another part of me loved it and pursued it. I would resolve not to do it anymore only to give in at the slightest temptation, seeking the comfort it seemed to offer. It was all a fantasy, offering instant gratification instead of demands and expectations, but now my real world is in shreds. It was all for free, but I am now paying a very heavy price. I have no money, no prospects, no friends, no options. What do fired pastors do next?

If only I could go back in time and change everything, I would, but now it's too late. Just one week! That's all I'd need to go back, to be open with you, to make things right before they went so horribly wrong. I never really thought I'd be caught out. I thought I'd always have time to make this change or that. But that kind of thinking can't go on forever, and it goes back an awful long way. I guess it's obvious that I should never have started to look at that stuff, but as I see things from this perspective I see other failures as well, even bigger ones. I needed to deal with things in ways that weren't destructive. I needed to reach out to others earlier. I'm so very sorry. You were my one effort to do that and all I've succeeded in doing is dragging you into my mess. All I see as I look around me are the people I've hurt. I've failed in almost every way. The pain and grief and regret are nearly unbearable.

Guard your heart, Dan. I didn't guard mine.

Sam

Daniel Donford

From:	danield@charis.net
Sent:	Tuesday 10 February, 3:16 p.m.
To:	eldon@charis.net
Subject:	Dismay

Dear Uncle Eldon,

Sam Campbell, my pastor friend from across town, is no longer a pastor. He's been fired. Over the last few years he's been increasingly caught up in an addiction to internet pornography and now it has been exposed.

You can imagine that he is heartbroken. I can almost weep when I think of the damage he's done. His wife Barbara doesn't want to have anything to do with him at the moment. Apparently the story has made it into the local paper, so the image of Christians has taken another battering. His reputation has been ruined and he's worried his children will be taunted at school. His church has been brought to its knees. Now he has to rebuild his whole life. He is a broken, broken man.

I know that because he's sitting in our lounge right now. Barbara couldn't face having him in their home so we invited him to come and stay with us for a while. It will give her time to think, and him an opportunity to begin to gather himself together.

It's very sobering. I can now see more clearly than ever how good your advice was to build boundaries. I've not been caught up in what Sam was, but I've put filters on my internet. I'm going to ask Stafford to keep me accountable, and I'm never going to surf the web with the door closed. I don't think it helped that Sam was able to use his computer without anyone looking over his shoulder.

It's almost funny. There were so many times when I wanted to turn my back on pastoral ministry. An experience like this has shown me just how precious it is, and how I want to hold onto it. I don't want to be derailed like Sam. I'll do all I can to prevent that from ever happening!

But right now I could do with your advice. How do I go about counselling Sam? Have you encountered anything like this before?

Dan

Uncle Eldon

From:	eldon@charis.net
Sent:	Wednesday 11 February, 11:01 a.m.
To:	danield@charis.net
Subject:	Re: Dismay

Dan:

I am saddened to hear of your pastoral friend who has re-vealed his addiction to pornography. It grieves me to hear of good men sidelined from ministry due to an inabil-ity or unwillingness to overcome temptation. During my ministry years I have been a part of many discipline and restoration situations of colleagues who had been caught in sin this way and who had ignored the warning signs and points of opportunity to change their ways. Maybe some of the things I have learned will be helpful as you come alongside your friend.

One thing I notice after a lifetime of observing pastors fail in a variety of ways is that not once has there been evidence of deliberate destruction. In other words, I know of no man who got out of bed one morning and decided to engage in behaviour that will destroy his ministry. As you rightly indicate, it often starts with a sense of loneliness and isolation brought on by the pressures and expectations of others. Consciously or unconsciously, there can arise in the heart of the Pastor a sense of entitlement for relief: 'I deserve to be a little self-centred because they don't realize how hard ministry is and how different are the pressures I face from regular working men.' That leads to what I would call 'brinkmanship'. It can take many forms – flipping through a magazine in a back corner of a bookstore, flirting with a waitress or store attendant – behaviour that when reviewed at the end of the day has had no discernible negative impact; it has brought no fire from heaven. So the next day they start where they left off and go a little bit further with still no harm done, no finger-pointing Elders. And so it goes, and with it comes numbness to reality, failure to see the edge of the cliff. What began with an apparently incidental and innocent event is suddenly exposed and the Pastor is gone.

On later review, all agreed they had been acting out brinkmanship, believing they were invincible and would never be caught. All could identify a tipping point where their emotional and physical energy was transferred from their spouse to this new 'relationship'. They felt some initial guilt and shame, but this was soon replaced by feelings of excitement and grandeur that sometimes produced anger towards their spouse. Sadly, none had taken the time to review the state of their marriage to identify why they had started down this destructive path. They were surely aware of the strains that the demands of pastoral ministry can place on a marriage, but it seems they were unwilling to take the high road of reinvestment in the vows they had made before God. One of the lessons they never learned is that a strong marriage is the best preventative against this kind of behaviour.

I also noticed that all these men expressed relief when their sin was brought into the light and they recognized the trap they had fallen into, yet surprisingly very few gave evidence of true repentance. Remorse at having their failure made public seemed to be the main source of their tears. A very low percentage had any further interest in ministry, and some saw their marriage disintegrate within a few years. But there were also those who faced their sin and truly repented, who worked successfully to restore a right relationship with the Lord and those around them. In doing so they found the words of David's Psalm to be true: 'A broken and contrite heart, O Lord, you will not despise.'

Dan, it is almost certain that your friend's needs right now are beyond your capacity to meet. But he needs you to bring words of grace and hope; he needs to know that while he has lost so much in recent days he has not lost your friendship and support. Your presence is enough, you don't need solutions or even advice, and he certainly does not need more judgment.

Go in the spirit of Galatians 6: 'If your brother is caught in a sin, you who are spiritual restore him gently.' Restoring gently does not mean restoring softly. He needs to be confronted with the full extent of his failure and the enormity of the consequences. Don't let him minimize the sin and criticize the punishment. 'Those the Lord loves He chastens', and only full confession can lead to full restoration. Hippocrates was the Greek physician and philosopher who gave us the Hippocratic Oath that all doctors are required to take. As you'd expect, he also left us with some wise observations on health and sickness. He said 'healing is a matter of time', and 'extreme remedies are needed for extreme conditions'. Your friend Sam needs time and he may well need some extreme remedies.

These extreme remedies will almost certainly include professional help, and the willingness to be absolutely transparent and honest with those most affected. He also needs what you can provide: redirection of his heart and mind towards God so that he can join in another aspect of David's prayer: 'Create in me a pure heart, O God, and renew a steadfast spirit within me. Restore to me the joy of your salvation and grant me a willing spirit, to sustain me.'

Be assured of my prayers as you do this, may grace and peace flow from you.

Eldon

PS, Given the friendship you were developing as couples, I am sure Hayley will be looking to support Sam's wife during this time of devastation for her. This could be the most difficult situation Barbara will face as a wife of a minister and she will need a confidential ear as she works through a variety of emotions. She is being forced to accept a situation she did not create, and her only immediate choice is how she will react to what has been dealt to her. First reactions are rarely a true reflection of who she is as a woman of God called with her spouse to serve in ministry. Most often there will be anger and the expressed desire to have him dealt with severely for the 'pain and shame he has brought on me'. Then with the prospect of a lost job and no income, she may quickly turn to blaming the church for its perceived lack of care and accountability. My advice for Hayley is to listen, offer personal comfort, and encourage her to trust God and the Elders to walk a path that with time will bring the best outcome for both Pastor and congregation. Walk with her for this day and then for the next. Time will reveal her true character and I am confident it will reveal a woman who trusts God and can ultimately display His attitudes of forgiveness and restoration of trust.

Daniel Donford

From: danield@charis.net
Sent: Thursday 19 February, 3:12 p.m.
To: eldon@charis.net
Subject: Prevention Is Better Than Cure

Dear Uncle Eldon,

Thanks for your advice about what to say to Sam. I've certainly seen the wisdom in what you offered and I've tried to follow it as best I can. It has helped that the full weight hasn't fallen on me, since Sam has started formal counselling sessions once a week. He hasn't told me everything about those, but they already seem to have identified some important issues in his life that even he wasn't aware of. It's amazing how interconnected everything is.

And that got me thinking. I look at Sam's life and the dramatic implosion is more than obvious. What's much less obvious is where it actually began. A lot of it will have to do with a series of destructive choices that led him deeper into sin. Some of it will go back to his childhood and his early formation. And some of it will reflect how he was shaped in ministry. I think he suffered from not having anyone like you in his life, or at least someone that he could open up to. I wonder now if the result would have been quite different had he put some things in place early on, but I'm not exactly sure what those things might be.

So here's my question, how can I make sure that I don't end up following Sam's experience? What might cause me to fall may be quite different in nature from what Sam faced, but I still might be wise to think in the same general terms of how to prevent any sort of fall in the first place. You've lasted the distance in ministry – how have you made sure to finish well by making the right sort of decisions and creating the right sort of rhythms and structures in the beginning? I know you've already given me so much advice that will touch on this, but are there any important lessons you can distil?

Dan

Uncle Eldon

From: eldon@charis.net
Sent: Friday 20 February, 11:57 a.m.
To: danield@charis.net
Subject: Re: Prevention Is Better Than Cure

Dan:

I am pleased to hear that Sam is taking steps to rebuild his life and my prayer will be that he does not give up on what will be a long but redemptive journey if he sees it through. It is amazing to me that God never gives up on us and even offers to redeem what was lost through our foolishness in walking away from His path for us.

You ask how you can guard against falling into the same destructive patterns and your implication is that I have it worked out and am cruising towards the finishing line. Believe me, it is not that easy. It is important even now that I run the race with the objective of finishing well.

The key words for me these days are from Proverbs 4:23: 'Guard your heart for it is the wellspring of life.' So simple and so direct, I must guard my heart if I am to know a full life that finishes well.

There is no question that the enemy of our souls will work hard to divert us from the path God has for us as spiritual leaders, and he doesn't need to have us fall to some major addiction to achieve his victory. His outcomes are realized when he can disconnect our heart and mind from the One we say we follow with full allegiance. So surfing the web, stopping to play some games, doodling through the sports results, reading the gossip pages, while not wrong in themselves, are sufficient to take our mind and heart away from listening and responding to the Lord. And in such a place we become more vulnerable to temptation.

I agree with all the books I have read on this subject that we are most vulnerable when we are hurt or angry or lonely or tired (they mention we should do an h-a-l-t checklist when stress is around). You well know that these things are too often a part of a Pastor's life. I am very familiar with the sequence: lonely or angry I allow my mind to wander and my heart becomes unguarded, exposed, and temptation appears.

Temptation seems to thrive on secrecy and secrecy leads to silence, so I must quickly counter with transparency and accountability to avoid my mind blurring or blotting out the consequences of the path I am thinking about. One way of pre-empting the success of temptation is to take time when the mind is clear to write down my strengths and weaknesses in terms of character and emotional stability (brutal honesty is needed with the help of a good spouse!). That has helped me identify the times of opportunity the enemy might find and the types of things he might offer, so that armed and ready I can be in a better position to stand against the 'fiery darts of the evil one'.

The bottom line for any of us will always be the willingness and ability to say 'no' to even the small and seemingly harmless things that would divert my heart and mind. So in case you haven't heard me say it recently, 'fix your eyes on Jesus'.

Please don't think that this is an issue only for young men like you. I have to confess that temptation to sin doesn't fade with age. Younger men may have more opportunities to actually engage in some very destructive behaviour, whereas that is less likely for someone my age. But what I do have is a mind that when alone and unchecked is capable of imagining despicable things. How good it would be to erase that tape, but the images remain to return at those times of hurt and loneliness. Even so, I can testify that God is able to transform by the renewing of my mind as I linger in His Word and fix my eyes on Him. That brings comfort and hope.

Start to prepare yourself today, Dan. Guard your heart so you can stand strong and finish well. Please pray that for me also.

Eldon

Daniel Donford

From:	danield@charis.net
Sent:	Monday 9 March, 8:32 a.m.
To:	eldon@charis.net
Subject:	Drama

Dear Uncle Eldon,

You won't credit what happened yesterday. I rang to tell you about it, but Aunt Ethel said that you're not feeling too well (I hope you're up and about soon). So I guess I'll have to resort to the usual email. It will hardly do justice to the drama of the moment, but I'll do my best!

It happened near the start of my sermon. I thought things were going okay, really. Admittedly, Meredith Bellweather dropped the communion cup, leaving a vivid stain down the front of her dress. She looked like she'd been stabbed! But the episode brought us all together – we had a gentle laugh and moved on. I thought my sermon began well enough. At the moment we are working through the life of David. I was talking about the story of Absalom in 2 Samuel 15. I had this rather apt illustration, which I was beginning to develop, when Tony Murkowski cut me short.

Out of nowhere, he just stood up – a brooding, dark presence in the second-to-back row. At first I thought he was heading off to the restroom, but he just stood there. The look he gave me chilled my extremities. I have never seen such a depth of enmity in another person. And this in the middle of church! He looked at me, but he didn't speak to me – he spoke to everyone else. He claimed that someone had to take a stand, that character issues in the leadership were not being addressed (he then waved airily in my direction) and if the Elders weren't going to do anything about it, then he would.

By now I was struggling just to stand up. I had an icy dread in the pit of my stomach. Visions of the church community physically tossing me out the door fluttered around in my head like distracting moths. I think my heart stopped beating. I was technically dead, I know it.

Then things got really interesting. He said that many other people in the church felt the same way, and that they would stand with him. No one did. Not one. Eleanor made a half-hearted effort to stand beside her husband, but lost confidence just as her knees began to straighten. I've never seen her look so lost. Tony looked straight at Harry Compton as if he expected him to stand and he very nearly did. But I think he could see that no one else was moving and then he looked at me with the strangest expression. I still can't read what it meant, but he'd obviously come to some decision. He stayed where he was, eyes fixed on the floor.

Tony's face was a sheet of black anger. He made some comment that if this was the state of God's church, he wanted no part of it. Endless, awkward silence: it must have been only a few seconds, but it felt like minutes. Then he demanded that if no one else was going to join him in his stand, he would go through that door (he stabbed his finger at the exit) and not come back. More silence. Then someone muttered under their breath – strangely, I couldn't tell who it was, either Doris Blackmore or Harold Carmichael (I'd never noticed before just how similar their voices are) – that if he was going to leave, he should just leave.

At that point Tony's complexion was a shade of red that bordered almost on blue. He swept his gaze across the congregation in typically imperious fashion. He grabbed Eleanor's hand and yanked her to her feet. Then quietly, so quietly I could hardly hear him, he said, 'I shake the dust off my feet. I turn my back on you all.' And then they were gone.

Well. Forget the sermon. What to do next? How to reassure people? I think it helped that I was struck by a thought as the Murkowskis walked out the door. It occurred to me then, that in all the time they had been back in the church I had never had a single conversation with them. I think I instinctively avoided them. Not once had I taken the opportunity to talk with them, to understand them, to reach them. Perhaps it would have made absolutely no difference to this day. Maybe their departure was inevitable. But I felt I had to take at least some responsibility. All along I had let others do the talking over these 'character issues'. In seeking to avoid conflict I had only prolonged it. And I had asked others to bear a burden that was really mine. I had put them into situations of conflict so that I didn't have to face it. More than that, to use your image, the Murkowskis' train had never moved. They got off in exactly the same condition that they got on. They had been under my care all this time and never challenged, never changed. I felt that I had let so many people down, including them, by not confronting them at the very beginning.

I felt it was important to own all these recognitions, but they didn't crush me. The first thing I was inclined to do was pray, and I did. I led the people in prayer for the Murkowskis, that God would show them grace, that if they really were gone they might find a church community that will help them to grow in their faith. Then I opened myself up to the congregation, these people who have become my dearest friends. I admitted that my character is not always what it should be, and I thanked them for their grace towards me in the past and, I was sure, in the future. I invited them to share the journey of our common growth together. All of this took several minutes and by then the atmosphere had changed completely. There were quite a few tears around the place. Martha Krinks, who really is a dear, stepped out of her seat to give me a hug. At that moment I felt like I was in the right place, that I truly belonged. My identity was being formed, not around the success or otherwise of my ministry (I was too conscious of my weakness for that) but around the grace of God in my life and in this community.

But all that still left the Murkowskis very much outside. I felt for them, I really did. I could imagine them living the rest of their lives without a church community, and I didn't want that to happen. The extent of my failure to engage with them became more and more apparent to me. So I hurried away from church and, swallowing my fear, went straight around to their house to see if we could talk. I hardly knew what I could possibly say. I guess I hoped that by opening up with each other we might have understood each other. That was naïve, I suppose. I know they were home, but they refused to answer the door. I tried calling last night but Eleanor just hung up the phone. I might give it a week or so and try them again, though I fear that nothing will help. I will carry my failure with me, and I can only hope it hasn't been too costly for them.

Do you have any perspective on all this?

Dan

Martha Krinks

From: martha_krinks@endora.com
Sent: Monday 9 March, 9:56 a.m.
To: jdandemtrout@vmail.org
Subject: Yesterday

Dear Janice,

You will not believe what happened in church yesterday, you really will not. I can hardly believe it myself. I have never seen anything like it. Right there in the middle of Daniel's sermon (and it was going so well, he is such a lovely preacher) that Tony Murkowski (who has been causing so much trouble for dear, young Daniel for months and months) stood up and practically dared the church to make him the pastor. Well! Everyone was really quite stunned. Of course no one wanted to do anything of the sort, not with Daniel leading us in the way he does with that sweet determination of his. So Tony stormed out of the church just like that and I doubt he will be back and between you and me I rather hope he does not come back. He has been nothing but trouble, that man.

I think we were all in a state of shock but dear Daniel brought us back to focus on the Lord so beautifully. I really have to almost laugh to think how far that young man has come in the time he's been our pastor. He is a different man now. The way he opened himself up to the church yesterday and humbled himself and admitted his failings and urged us all on was really just inspiring. I just had to praise the Lord for all that he has done. Because really I do think that the church has come a long way as well. We all have. People have found their niche. They are doing things they would not have even thought about doing a year ago. We've been set to work for the cause of God's Kingdom and what a sight it is to see! I know that it is God who causes these things to grow but he uses people to do it and I have to say that he has used Daniel to do it. I know he seemed so unpromising to others when he started but I always said he had the makings of a fine pastor and look at him now!

So I did what I have been wanting to do ever since he arived. I got out of my seat and I gave him a great big hug. You know I think he really appreciated it. We all laughed and cheered then we got on with what we were there to do. Have you ever heard anything like it? I couldn't have made it up if I tried. It was really quite wonderful.

Give my love to Ed.

Martha

Harry Compton

From: hjcompton@compton.com
Sent: Tuesday 10 March, 4:59 p.m.
To: murkowskis@griblet.org
Subject: Re: Betrayal

Tony,

I don't know why you're so upset with me. It's not like I was the only one who stayed in my seat. Everyone did! I know I was the one who brought you in, but I didn't see how badly you'd handle things. I didn't see that Dan would turn out okay.

You know what? I think I'm happy with the way things are.

Don't come back.

Harry

Uncle Eldon

From:	eldon@charis.net
Sent:	Thursday 12 March, 4:38 p.m.
To:	danield@charis.net
Subject:	Re: Drama

Dan:

Reading your email I have to say I am glad I was not there to take your phone call the other day. Having you write it down gives me time to think about a response, but it has also required you to reflect on what actually happened that Sunday. And as I reflect on your reporting of that day, I think I can see just what God has been doing in you and how far you've come.

If you have kept a record of our interaction over the period you have been at the church, it would be good to go back and look at how that interaction has changed. My recollection is that you arrived at Broadfield Community Church with a lot of good ideas and intentions but not much of a clue as to how they might be knit into the congregational life. You hit early roadblocks, causing your early mail to me to be punctuated by desperate cries for help. You had a few highs and many lows, but you stayed on task. Now your emails are marked by new words, words that are consistent with one who is a maturing life-long learner.

I'm glad you put aside the sermon, glad you prayed for the people who were causing you pain, and thankful you followed that prayer by facing the congregation with honesty, humility and transparency. The modern writers are calling that 'self awareness' and I have to say I would not have used those words to describe you a year or so ago. You invited the people to continue to share the journey together and I have a hunch they will. A leader like you have become is very easy to trust and follow. God has used this outwardly negative experience to reveal what He has been doing inwardly in your heart. I predict a new fulfilling chapter of ministry is starting for you.

That thought is reinforced by your report of going immediately to the Murkowskis' home to seek reconciliation. They were wise not to open the door. They are angry people and their behaviour in church was inappropriate and inexcusable. If the door had opened you would have been greeted either by more venom or with spluttered and ill-prepared words of justification. Neither would have added value to the situation.

I suggest you spend several days praying earnestly for a softening in their hearts, and for the Lord to open a door for you to have a natural opportunity to talk with them and ask for a meeting in the future where you can express sadness for your attitudes. Take it from there. One of the consequences of having never visited them in their home while they were members, is that it is highly unlikely you will be invited to their home under these circumstances and even if you are, there is no memory at the meeting of a previous visit in happier times. The objective at this stage is to de-escalate (remember that word?) their negative views towards you and the church.

Through all this I thank God for you, Dan, and for the way He has worked in your life through the events at Broadfield. Would you thank Him too, and ask Him to keep your heart soft towards Him and softer towards the people you serve, even the difficult ones?

God Bless You.

Eldon

Daniel Donford

From:	danield@charis.net
Sent:	Thursday 19 March, 4:53 p.m.
To:	eldon@charis.net
Subject:	Sam

Dear Uncle Eldon,

I'm sure you'll remember the tragedy of Sam Campbell's pastoral career. Some weeks on from the initial detonation it is now definitely over. It seems that no one else is interested in acting as his advocate so I have been involved in conversations with his Elders. The question is not whether Sam can be given his role back. Personally, I would have thought it should be at least a possibility after an appropriate period of counselling, repentance and rehabilitation. Surely the church, of all places, should demonstrate the promise of forgiveness and reconciliation, of grace to the undeserving.

But the Elders there won't hear a word of it. You'll recall a man named Mervin had been causing some problems for Sam with his undermining criticisms. Well, he seems to be in the driving seat now and he is even more unnerving and domineering than Sam had made out. Apparently he sees himself offering the church the kind of leadership it has long been lacking. I stood up to him in our meetings, to all of them. 'He who is without sin…' and all that. I asked them if they had never felt the same sort of temptation that Sam faced, if they had never given in or imagined in their own minds doing things that were even worse. They had the good grace to let their eyes drop at that point, but they still wouldn't budge.

A new tone has been set and Sam is out. The message is pretty clear – he is not welcome, not even in the very back pew. I find the whole thing unspeakably sad. Sam's sin has very quickly spiralled his church into (I think) a most unhealthy place. I'm not sure it will ever recover.

His own life is still a complete mess, but there are some promising signs. Barbara has agreed to go to counselling with him, so that's something, though that's the only context in which she's prepared to speak to him. He's still living with us, while Hayley spends some time most days driving across town to chat with Barbara. It amazes us just how few true friends they had in the end. What friendships they enjoyed have been exposed as extremely fragile. Perhaps it was really only their role that attracted those seeming friends in the first place. Now that it has collapsed, they have gone too. I can't help thinking that isolation was part of the problem.

So Sam is no longer a pastor. Who knows if he ever will be again in some other place? One good thing is that he has found another job. He's working as a storeman at one of the big supermarkets near here. He says he's finally putting his height to good use. It may not be nearly as rewarding as his former vocation but at least it gives him something to focus on, and apparently he's finding some of the changes quite refreshing. It seems that his new workmates are more understanding and generous than his old congregation.

You know, the whole thing is a disaster. I wouldn't wish any of this on anyone. But there's something special about representing God's grace in the midst of sin and chaos. And I think I can hope that Sam's future is not quite as bleak as he first thought.

Dan

Daniel Donford

From:	danield@charis.net
Sent:	Saturday 4 April, 10:37 p.m.
To:	eldon@charis.net
Subject:	Wedding

Dear Uncle Eldon,

It's been a great day! I know it's late but I still want to tell you about it.

I've taken my first wedding! Two Sundays ago Meredith and Harold announced their engagement. I can't say I was too surprised by that – the signs had been there for a long time. And once they'd made the decision there was no point in waiting. They sure are old enough to know their own minds. So old, in fact, as Meredith herself said, that if the engagement period was too long, one or other of them was likely to die in the middle of it. So we all hurried around and helped them to make some plans. It was a pretty simple arrangement in the end, but I found it particularly meaningful.

One reason for that is that it's the first time I've married another couple. I must say they are hardly what I had in mind when I imagined my first set of newlyweds, but that didn't matter at all. Just like any bride and groom they are mightily in love and rejoicing in God's gracious providence in giving them each other. Harold seems positively besotted. His good eye is trained on Meredith whenever she's around. They plan to sell his home and live in hers, for the sake of the cats. Rather him than me, but I think they'll do well. They're away for a couple of nights on a short honeymoon (they made it brief so as to offend feline sensibilities as little as possible), then they will move in on Monday. No, I'm not at all worried for them. It's Harold's dog I worry about: a one-eyed, diminutive canine up against eighteen cats. I don't think it stands a chance.

Yet the day was important for more than just their own happiness, as deep and as special as it is. I also gained a new sense of my own place in things, one that gave me a deeper appreciation for the lives of those around me. It's possible to trace this wedding today all the way back to that afternoon when I first met Meredith. As much as I thought it was an entirely forgettable experience at the time, that encounter eventually blossomed into today's delight and joy. I was allowed to play a part in that story, and that is just one life. In other words, what I do is important because people are important.

I saw that as well as I looked out over the congregation, which was made up mostly of our own church members. I hope this won't sound too grandiose, but today I caught a passing glimpse of the majesty of each human being, their depth, their soul. For sure, I have seen the squalor that is fallen human nature in my time at Broadfield, but I've also seen the richness of every life that seems so ordinary and mundane on the surface. Go a little deeper and there's a lot going on. God has given me a special place in that 'going on'. I now cherish my role far more than I used to. I thought of that as I considered the people sitting in the auditorium. Sam had invited Barbara to come with him and she agreed. It's the first time they've done anything together (except for counselling). Hopefully something in the nature of the day reminded them both of the enduring force of their own marriage covenant. And

I found it exhilarating to speak the words to Harold and Meredith: 'By the authority vested in me I now pronounce you husband and wife.' I felt like I was speaking the very words of life. That is what today was about, life itself, and I saw it from a new angle.

And it was a day about our church. The weather was perfect for a wedding and the auditorium was flooded with sunlight and filled with people. My first memories of serving in the building seem a whole lot darker. That's probably just the associations, but today I realized the extent of tangible change that we had achieved together. The building is different, but more importantly, so are we.

After the reception Meredith and Harold organized a dance. The theme was music from the Forties, when they were children. The music seemed foreign to our younger ears but it was so much fun. Hayley and I didn't know what we were supposed to be doing but we had a lot of laughs doing it. In the quieter tunes we danced close and spoke softly. We talked about us and our own marriage, about our life and the children, about our ministry in this place. Hayley commented how far I'd come in the time we'd been here. We agreed that Broadfield has been good for us. I didn't always see it that way, but I see it now.

I'm grateful to God. I really do believe that all our trials and sufferings are of little account once we see how big the picture really is.

Well, I'd better go. Hayley is calling me to bed. But it's so good to have you around to report to. I'm not sure where I'd be without you.

Dan

Progressions

Daniel Donford

From:	danield@charis.net
Sent:	Thursday 23 April, 8:52 a.m.
To:	eldon@charis.net
Subject:	What To Say?

Dear Uncle Eldon,

I'm stuck at my computer hardly knowing which key to hit. I'm just not sure what to say. I'm sorry that I found so few words on the phone last night as well. I can't quite remember now, but I think I might have tried to put on a brave face, which would hardly have helped. 'Terminal cancer'. 'Rapid progression'. The words are chilling, even now. Truth to tell, I was embarrassed by my own lack of faith and my selfishness. I quickly allowed myself to imagine a world in which I was bereft of your support and presence. I couldn't see past my own potential loss to glimpse the majesty and the surety of God's purposes, God's grace. Then I spent too long wallowing in the shock of what this might mean for me. But finally, in the early hours of the morning, I at last began to think of how this must be for you and Aunt Ethel. I was in awe of your faith. I am still so impressed by your fortitude, your sense of God's presence and generosity, your confidence in the hand of God in this broken, often bitter world. Once again, your example has lifted me up and carried me forward.

So here I am, wanting to do all I can to share this next season of your journey with you. I don't know what the end will be. I don't know how many more seasons there are beyond this one, for any of us. But I do know I want to be there for you, just as you have been there for me.

I can recall a piece of advice you gave me once, about pastoral visits. Act normal, you said. When a person's life is in crisis, one of the best gifts you can give is a brief moment in which life seems to be normal, almost as it once was, an assurance that no matter how much changes around us, not all is lost. So I'm going to follow your advice. Perhaps it will help us both. Here I am, acting normal.

So let me talk about life here for a while. Ever since the wedding I've had the sense that the church has entered into a new season. The winds of God's Spirit are clearly blowing through, filling our sails. I have to say that Larry has been one of the highlights. He's irrepressible in his new faith. There's a new light in his eyes, his life has clearly been realigned, and people are coming to faith all around him. Rosie was the first. She says their marriage has been renewed. For the first time, she doesn't feel like she's in second place to everything else. It was enough to start her asking questions, looking for answers. She had coffee with Clive's wife, Lois, seven straight mornings in a row. On the seventh day she came to faith, she rested from all her works – it was all very poetic and biblical. This was the first time that Lois had ever led anyone to the Lord, so you can imagine that she and Clive have been transformed as well! Larry has opened up a whole new line of connections. Several of his friends have been coming to church; three so far have come to faith. Clive and Larry asked me if I would run a small group study for all of Larry's friends. I turned them down – said that they should do it instead. So they are. Clive and Lois are doing what they had never even conceived of before, and with amazing effectiveness.

Those three friends of Larry who came to faith did so in the course of their group!

One other thing I'm pleased about is that some of those friends are couples my own age. Along with a few others who have joined Broadfield lately, Hayley and I finally have some friends in our own stage of life. It feels like a major gap in the church has been filled, like we are now more complete in a way that God wants us to be. I think it's positive and healthy. We're growing.

The new physical environment has helped far more than I thought it would. I think we reworked the mental walls when we extended the physical ones. But it's more than just changing a building: there's new life everywhere we look. After a long winter the church is finally in a season of spring. It's like the potential that was locked away inside the church has been broken open, just like the expensive perfume that was poured on the feet of Jesus. The aroma is life-giving. Everyone can see the difference, and no one would want to go back to the way things were. All the sacrifices have been worth it, just to see this.

It's not perfect, of course. I never did get to talk to the Murkowskis — they flat out refused to see me. Nothing I did would make them budge. So I will just have to make the best of that situation, recalling the lessons I learned and praying for them now and then. I know this is not the last time I'll go through an experience like that. People leave churches, sometimes badly, and there will be times when I will have to bear some responsibility for that. But I think my heart is bigger than it was, more seasoned. I hope I'll do a better job of things in the future. That said, I'm very glad not to be experiencing conflict right now!

Everyone is excited – it's not just me. There's even talk of a bigger building. I think that not so long ago I might have been carried away with people's enthusiasm. I'm happy to hear it, but I'm no longer content to locate my identity in the size of the congregation, the shape of the building. All I want to do is be faithful to the story God is telling in this place, right now. If that means a bigger building, I'll give myself to the cause. But if not, I'll be content with whatever God has in store for me.

Which brings me back to your news. Having told you mine, I am strangely encouraged. The purposes of God are beyond all knowing, but I can trust his wisdom and his goodness, even now, even in the face of your cancer. I hope you might have found some little encouragement in all of that as well, though I can imagine I needed to see it much more than you did!

Dan

Uncle Eldon

From: eldon@charis.net
Sent: Saturday 25 April, 3:34 p.m.
To: danield@charis.net
Subject: Re: What To Say?

Dan:

My heart overflows with thankfulness to God as I read your last email and as I think back over the time you have been sharing with me your journey into pastoral leadership. What changes God has brought to your life and what blessing God has accomplished in the lives of so many because of your faithfulness to Him. I agree – your heart has grown, and it warms this old man's heart to see it. Through pain and tears, He has shaped you into a mature man of God, and I am confident that having begun that good work, He will carry it to completion. Continue to follow Him and you will finish well.

Thank you for your concerns for me. You allude to my terminal cancer and that is what they are saying about my condition. But while we both know what they mean, we also know that in the end it won't be cancer that gets me but God who calls me into His presence. For God is greater than any bodily condition, He is not confined by any process of bodily cells, He is the Lord. And He is moving me now to a stage of life when I will forever live in His presence and forever be free of pain, disease, and tears. My strength is failing, but my joy is increasing at the thought that soon it will be no longer faith, but sight. It will be worth it all, to see Jesus.

Sleep patterns are changing so there are long periods when I am alone and awake. I enjoy these times with the Lord, and also take the time to review His goodness through my life. He has been faithful; I hope He sees the same in me. Sometimes I wonder what of me will last, if my life has had any significance to others. The last few years have showed me how fleeting is success, how control and influence can quickly shrink away, and how futile are the efforts to hold on to things that are not eternal.

You know my love of the Old Testament and the stories of God leading His people. Of the way His Word reveals not only the strengths but also the weaknesses and humanness of even the patriarchs. So I am no longer afraid to acknowledge my weaknesses and acknowledge God's grace through my failures. I find myself often crying out with the Psalmist to a God who knows and understands, and who will welcome me into His presence soon.

'There is a time for everything' and I am not afraid of what is ahead. I am at peace with God, it is well with my soul.

Eldon

Daniel Donford

From:	danield@charis.net
Sent:	Wednesday 27 May, 9:23 p.m.
To:	eldon@charis.net
Subject:	A Good Day

My dear, dear Uncle Eldon,

I know you're gone. I know you're well beyond the reach of any email. I know all that, and yet I can't stop sending them, not yet. Your decline has been too rapid, your departure too quick, your absence too great. I don't know who will read this message. Maybe no one. It doesn't matter. There are still too many things left to say. If only I had more time, more words. So here I am back at my keyboard, pretending that you're still around to reply, to offer me one more instalment of advice that will inevitably lift my spirits, fire my courage and provoke my awe and gratitude.

'Thank you!' seems so trite and ineffectual, but where else to begin? The list of debts is long and overwhelming, but perhaps the greatest was today. How can I possibly repay it? Asking me to take your funeral was the highest honour I have ever been given. Uncle Eldon, it was magnificent! It gave me a much deeper glimpse into your life and service for the Kingdom, and taught me again what that service is all about: people. Your funeral today was stacked full of people. We couldn't fit them all in. We found the biggest auditorium we could and that wasn't enough. People stood shoulder to shoulder at the sides, they filled the foyer and overflowed out into the parking lot where we set up speakers. It brought home to me that a life of influence and a life well lived is known by the people who are touched and changed along the way. Today's celebration was a visible testament to your life, not in its material success but in its personal, spiritual, eternal impact.

It made me think about the kind of funeral I want to have when my time comes: one like yours. One where life and tears and joy and sadness and gratitude all overflow and intermingle. One where people can't stop talking about the impact you've had on their life. I know you didn't ask for this, but we had an open floor at one point, so that people could share their memories and reflections. I'm glad we did. It went on for over an hour! It didn't feel like that. No one talked for too long. No one focused on themselves. They all spoke of you, and how God had used you to shape their experience of him. I'm glad we got it all on video, because I couldn't possibly remember it all now. The list seems endless. The teenager who got pregnant – you showed her such grace and compassion. The family whose husband and father ran out on them – you offered practical support and hope. The guy you found lying in the gutter, stoned, who is now, six years later, an Elder in his church. The father of three who grew up under your teaching: his faith and understanding would have been so much the poorer without your steady, faithful input over the years, and he tries every day to live out all that you passed on as he brings up his family. You taught him how to live! Even the elderly woman whose faltering, frail voice we could barely hear, who lived for Thursday afternoons when you always came round to pay her a visit. The cab driver who followed you into church one Sunday morning simply because he sensed in you something he had never discerned in any other passenger in all his years of driving. I could go on and on. When I finally, reluctantly drew that section to a close I could barely talk. I can't recall ever being more deeply moved.

As you asked, there were two eulogies. Your old friend Malcolm spoke so eloquently about how you trained him for ministry. That was pretty mindboggling once I worked out that in addition to all the people you had influenced directly there was another large circle of influence that worked itself out through his own decades of ministry. And then I thought about me and my tiny contribution to the Kingdom – even that has your stamp on it. The far horizon of your influence was further than I could possibly see, once I began to layer up all these interconnected networks of significance.

Then Max Anderson shared with us what your leadership had done for the church over the decades, and he should know, being an Elder for the bulk of those years. He described how it had grown in every conceivable dimension, rarely through anything flashy and dramatic, but as a result of steady, loyal, unflinching and sacrificial leadership through all the seasons in the life of the church. Again I had the sense that lives had been fundamentally altered by something that bore your touch. I glimpsed the grace of God in allowing ordinary people a hand in crafting something that is truly powerful and magnificent.

In the midst of all the wonder and emotion I saw something else that I would never have conceived. I recall you saying that you were once just like me: struggling, weak and bewildered. But I never believed you. It seemed insane. Surely you were always this accomplished, this experienced, this capable. Today, Max painted a picture of your early years. He said that at one point things were just too difficult. You were on the verge of giving up. And then he paused, bent forward towards the microphone and whispered four words: 'Imagine if he had.' I was stunned. I saw it all so vividly. If you had abandoned your calling so early in the race, this funeral would have been so different and the lives of the people packed into that hall would never have been the same. And then I realized that I almost made that mistake. I don't know if my life will end up having the same influence (though I hope it will) but I am so grateful you didn't let me give up. Now I know why.

At the close of the service I painted a scene for people. It was so real to me, just at that moment. I described your entry into heaven. I imagined angels beyond number lining the roadway, cheering you on. And then the crowd parts and you see Jesus. He welcomes you home with arms outstretched. You see his scars, you remember your wounds, but they are as nothing now. He looks into your eyes with a nod of understanding, a warmth and approbation that goes deep into your deepest being. 'You did well', he says gently, though all hear the words. 'Very well.' At that moment all the burdens, the problems, the trials, the setbacks and the wounds of this earthly pilgrimage fade away into nothing, and now the full significance of what it all meant is unveiled. It was worth every tear, every exertion, and the return on your investment defies all description.

And so, Uncle Eldon, you kept teaching me to the end, even today. The lessons I've learned from you will stay with me always.

Because just as you were once like me, one day I want to be just like you.

Dan

Daniel Donford

From: danield@charis.net
Sent: Thursday 4 June, 11:22 a.m.
To: eldon@charis.net
Subject: Goodbye…

Dear Eldon,

This is difficult, but I think it's time for me to say goodbye, at least for now. I have to let you go. I'm sure going to miss these emails, your replies. They have meant
so much. I'd like to see if I can somehow capture that
meaning in one last message, even if I am the only one
to read it.

Where to start? These past two years might have been
the end of me, if not for your presence in the middle of
a near-endless stream of struggles and wounds and tri-
umphs and gains. You saved my life so often, and in doing that you made a difference to the life of our church.
Without once stepping through the door you made your
influence felt. Because of that, Broadfield is a community of much freer, generous people serving God in the
world, loving each other and loving their neighbours.
'The Lord has done this, and it is marvellous in our eyes.'
I marvel to think that I have been allowed to stand in
the middle and see it all happen around me. The church
is now so very different from when I first arrived, and
not because my initial plans were so beautifully imple-
mented. Hardly! I can laugh about it now, but really I was
so foolish. Yet people stuck with me, God entrusted me
with the task, and he gave me a priceless gift to help me
along: he gave me you.

I guess we will never grasp the full breadth of your impact in this world, though I'm sure by now you see it clearly. But I know, at least for me, what you have done in my life. It brings me to tears whenever I think about it. For all the wounds and the worries – and they were deep and heavy, I will never diminish what they cost – I would not have missed this experience for all the world. I shared something important and valuable, with the people in the congregation, with Hayley as we've served together, and with you as we've shared the journey. I think God has laid the foundation for something great. I now understand how you could minister in one place for forty years. I don't know if that's the way it will work out for me, and I really don't mind if it doesn't. All that matters is being faithful to the call of God on my life, wherever that leads. So whatever the future holds, the past couple of years have been important. I have an inkling this is only the beginning.

You have opened up that future and made it possible. I would never have survived without you to hold me steady. I could make a long list of the crises I faced and you threw a lifeline. You were there to tell me what was really going on, to say what I needed to hear and to offer endless patience and grace and encouragement to propel me forward.

And now you are not here. The gap is enormous, the effect could easily be paralyzing, except that I feel fortified and determined. I would have liked to have you around for so much longer, but I accept that cannot be. More than that, I see the need for me and my generation to take your place. Everyone needs an Eldon, and I want to be an Eldon to others. I want to be for them what you have been for me. I also want to live a life of influence, just like yours. I want to model the same steady perseverance you have shown. I want my life to count in the kind of ways that yours has counted. And for me, that means being a pastor. I know there are plenty of other vineyards to work in, but this is mine. It wasn't so long ago that I was afraid of it, daunted and intimidated. Now I see it clear-eyed, but not cowed. The position of pastor is one of sacrificial service in an environment that is bound to leave its bruises on the soul. But that is only because there is a corresponding potential to leave a powerful and lasting mark on the souls of others. The rewards far exceed the risks, as great as they are. And I think I'm ready to sign up for that service, having seen in your life the fruit it can bear in the lives of others.

Eldon, no one has shaped me more than you. I look back and see just how far I've come, and how much I've grown. I am the same man I was then, but different as well. I have been forged and seasoned. I have become so much more aware and alert, not just to the dangers and the potential without, but to those within. I think I am truly living in a way that I wasn't before. I have grown. And you have been the one to nurture me. I thank God for your life. I thank God for your contribution in my life. And I give myself to his service, praying that I might in time become half the man that you have been. If I come even close, I will be well pleased.

This is a precious, poignant moment. It hangs suspended in the air, poised in a sudden silence and stillness, like I'm holding my breath. What is required? A final sentence or a lifelong memory? Maybe both. I groan, and look forward to heaven when bereavements and farewells and departures are a forgotten order. Until then, I must bear them and honour them. And so, Eldon, until we meet again on the great and glorious day when the full story of all we've done is told…goodbye. You will be missed. You will not be forgotten. You have meant so much, to me and so many others. Goodbye, my friend. Goodbye.

Daniel